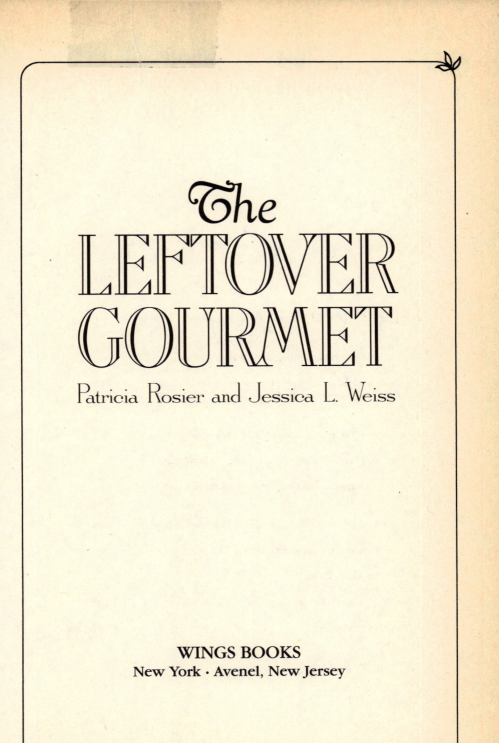

The
LEFTOVER
GOURMET

Patricia Rosier and Jessica L. Weiss

WINGS BOOKS
New York · Avenel, New Jersey

Copyright © 1991 by National Press Books, Inc.
All rights reserved.

This 1993 edition is published by Wings Books,
distributed by Outlet Book Company, Inc., a Random House Company,
40 Engelhard Avenue, Avenel, New Jersey 07001, by arrangement
with National Press Books, Inc.

Random House
New York • Toronto • London • Sydney • Auckland

Printed and bound in the United States of America

Library of Congress Cataloging-in-Publication Data

Rosier, Patricia.
        The leftover gourmet / Patricia Rosier & Jessica L. Weiss.
            p.   cm.
        Originally published: 1st ed. Bethesda, MD : National Press,
    c1991.
        Includes index.
        ISBN 0-517-08916-5
        1. Cookery (Leftovers)   I. Weiss, Jessica L.   II. Title.
    TX652.R6715   1993
    641.5'52—dc20   92-34867
                                                                     CIP

10 9 8 7 6 5 4 3 2 1

Dedication

My wife, Patricia Rosier, died January 15, 1986 at the age of 43, after an 8 month battle against lung cancer. Pat derived a lot of pleasure from caring for those around her. She had boundless energy, intelligence, and humor and devoted these qualities to creating a nourishing and nurturing home for her family. She felt there was no better way to show love than to provide sustenance, which she often did by delivering Meals-on-Wheels to the elderly. Her love affair with life was consistently linked to food. She loved excellence and was appalled at waste. When she began to cook, in high school, it was perfection she was striving for, and perfection she achieved, when she became a serious cook in her twenties.

Pat's never ending creative imagination, and her encompassing love were the secret ingredients that her family and friends consumed with delight in celebration of life. All of us who broke bread with her miss her smile.

Peter Rosier

Acknowledgments

There are number of people without whom *The Leftover Gourmet* could never have materialized. First, I must thank Alan Sultan and Rebekah Greenwald, who were by my side every step of the way. I would like to thank Dr. Peter Rosier, whose undying love for his wife and dedication to this project often provided essential inspiration. I would also like to thank Debby Malovany for her assistance with the book layout. And of course, a thanks to my mom, who taught me all I know about plate cleaning and making due with what you've got. Additionally, the following are amongst my favorite cookbooks. They have provided me with the necessary tools to complete *The Leftover Gourmet*.

James Beard's Theory and Practice of Good Cooking by James Beard in collaboration with Jose Wilson, Alfred A. Knopf, New York, 1984

The James Beard Cookbook by James Beard in collaboration with Isabel E. Callvert, Dell Publishing Co., Inc., 750 Third Avenue, New York, 1959

Mastering the Art of French Cooking by Julia Child, Alfred A. Knopf, New York, 1970

The New York Times Cookbook by Craig Clairborne with Pierre Franey, The New York Times Book Co., Inc., 3 Park Avenue, New York, 1975

The Joy of Cooking by Irma S. Rombauer and Marion Rombauer Becker, The Bobbs-Merrill Co., Inc., New York 1931

The Williams-Sonoma Cookboook and Guide to Kitchenware by Chuck Williams, Random House, Inc., New York, 1986

Table of Contents

Blue Cheese & Tomato Tart—Broccoli Quiche—Smoked Salmon
Quiche—Chicken & Mushroom Quiche—Omelette Introduction—
Basic Omelette—Curried Mushroom Omelette—Crabmeat Omelette—
Smoked Salmon Omelette—Salami & Cheese Omelette—Denver
Omelette—Panama Eggs—French Toast—Rich French Toast—Apple
Pancakes—Apple Muffins—Bran Muffins

Soup Introduction—Basic Broth or Soup Made From Bones—Turkey
Noodle Soup—Romaine Rice Soup—White Bean Soup—Faux
Gazpacho—Spreads Introduction—Pesto/Vegetable Cream Cheese
Spread—Nova Scotia Spread—Anchovy Cheese—Chicken Mousse—
Chopped Chicken Livers—Deviled Beef Spread—Beef Mousse—
Ham Mousse—Deviled Ham I—Deviled Ham II—Paté Introduc-
tion—Basic Beef Paté—Cold Cuts Paté—Chicken Paté—Paté
Maison—Achra—Rice Remick—Tuna Crisps—Pickled Fish—Beef
Rolls—Meat Turnovers—Salami Gougere

Florentine Fish—Hot Chicken/Turkey Timbale—Apricot Soy Chicken—Almond Chicken—Chicken/Turkey Elena—Chicken/ Turkey Tetrazzini—Spinach & Chicken Filled Manicotti—Rice & Beef Bake—Beef Stroganoff—Sliced Beef with Green Peppercorn Sauce— Dragon Fillet with Snow Peas—Lamb Stew—Curried Lamb with Apples—Lamb with Black Bean Sauce

Preface

My earliest memories of mealtimes are filled with references to the poor starving children in Europe. I consumed countless unwanted and unneeded calories because of the guilt I was made to feel if I ever "wasted" any food. How my becoming the best plate-cleaner in the family helped the poor starving devils in Europe remained a mystery, but in my younger years I simply assumed my mother knew something I didn't know and I felt a righteous pride in doing my part to help all those hungry kids. As I matured I never lost my respect for food, meals, or for the virtue of the clean plate.

Motherhood presented my next confrontation with the waste problem. I couldn't take the untouched French toast, pancakes, lamb chops (and all the other wholesome delights new mothers tend to force on unhungry little babies) from the high chair to the garbage pail. My own childhood training persisted and my mouth became the depository for all unwanted morsels of goodness. If only my mouth had been involved without my hips and stomach, the impetus for the creation of this book would never have come to be. I was cleaning plates six times each day — I had to do something!

I started my approach to the problem of waste scientifically. I saved everything that was leftover and "recycled" it into something else. The recycled meals were frequently superior to the originals. The aid of the blender, food processor, freezer, microwave oven and other kitchen tools now widely available, made it easy to reprocess foods and give them totally new identities.

The spiraling cost of food, combined with the wider availability of staples in supermarkets only added cogence to the "Don't throw it away" philosphy.

You Can Make Do ... Do Without ... Use It Up ... Wear It Out
— But Don't Throw It Away !

Patricia Rosier
Fort Myers, FL

Introduction

Although my background is extremely different from Patricia's, our sensitivity to starvation is very similar. My experiences traveling in Africa and Mexico, combined with my research on food habits in the United States and their relative impact on the environment, enhance my frustrations with living in as wasteful a society as I do. We waste 20 to 35% of the food we produce. Food wastes in 1990 comprised 7.9% of the total solid waste in our landfills. This means that over 13 million tons of wasted food are decomposing into methane gas, contributing to the demise of our ozone layer. Consider this, according to the American Institute of Food Distribution, there is an average of 1400 pounds of food available to every American each year. Based on this figure, the food we are wasting in this country alone could feed 18,571,428 people. When these numbers are taken into account, it seems almost criminal to waste what really is a precious commodity.

Another important reason to "recycle" food is that it saves money. If the average cost of feeding each person their 3.84 pounds of food per day is approximately $4.90 (excluding meals purchased outside of the home), and 1/4 to 1/3 of that money is literally being thrown out with the trash, the average family of four could save about $2,000 per year simply by utilizing their leftovers.

From a global perspective, saving the valuable resources that are used in the production and transportation of food helps to curtail the rapid destruction of our planet. According to the Worldwatch Institute, the average mouthful of food travels 1,300 miles from the farm where it is grown to your dining room table. By recycling your food to create just one extra meal, you can save the trucks and airplanes which carry the food thousands of miles in transportation and thousands of gallons of gasoline. Add to this the hundreds of thousands of dollars for the labor of the truckers and the cost of the vehicles, including their maintenance and repair. To top this out, there are the multitudinous pounds of carbon dioxide emitted by these vehicles which are a major contribution to the greenhouse effect and global warming. Consider as well the electricity used to keep the food fresh and the agricultural costs of producing the food in the first place. Not to mention the gravity of the problems posed by soil depletion, erosion, water pollution, and pesticides.

So, look at this cookbook as having dual purposes. Not only will you delight your family and friends with a plethora of exquisite meals, but you will also be doing your part to save our planet.
So grab your sauce pan,
and let's feed the world!

Jessica L. Weiss
Washington DC, 1991

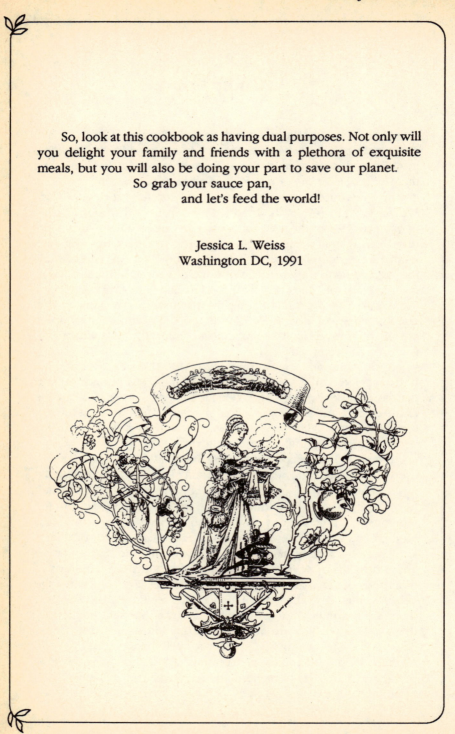

CHAPTER 1

Basics You Should Always Have Around

THINGS TO COME IN...
Basics You Should Always Have Around

EQUIPMENT

Cooking gourmet food does not necessarily require exotic or expensive equipment. It does however, require investing in a few good basic tools, which can be added to as you discover new areas into which you would like to venture. The following are some tips and a good list to start you on your way towards gastronomical success. And remember, attention to details can make or break a meal. Even the most simple of salads will benefit when served on a chilled plate with a chilled salad fork. Similarly, hot meat dishes should always be served on warmed plates, lest the fat or sauce coagulate into a lumpy mess on the side. Furthermore, atmosphere is crucial. I've always noticed that a great, oversized picnic blanket for the outdoors, or lots of candles burning on the dining room table have always somehow improved the taste and overall effect of a meal.

POTS & PANS

Pots and pans are your most basic tools, and as such, you should purchase them with great care. Good ones will cost more, but in the long run, it's definitely worth it. Choose pots of a fairly heavy gauge as they tend to diffuse heat more evenly. Be careful however, that the pots are not so heavy that they become awkward or burdensome to maneuver. Also choose pots with tight fitting lids that are heavy enough to stay in place over a boiling liquid, and pans with sturdy handles that are welded on. There is nothing worse than pulling a skillet off of the stove and having it crash to the floor while you are left holding the remnants of its handle. Handles of a hollow construction are good because they tend to remain much cooler than the pan itself. Also, try to get oven proof handles as they are much more practical in that you can keep dishes warm in the oven.

A good material for your basic pans is stainless steel with an aluminum inlay in the bottom, or heavy cast aluminum lined with stainless steel. These won't warp, and are easy to clean. For frying and baking pans, cast iron is a good choice. It is very durable, resists chipping, denting, and warping, and conducts heat slowly and evenly. However, you should not cook acidic food in them, and they need to be kept seasoned. Enameled cast iron does not need to be seasoned, but it is more likely to chip than regular cast iron, and should never be cleaned with bleach or anything more abrasive than a nylon sponge. Sheet steel is good when you need efficient, rapid heat conductivity, such as in a pasta boiling pot, or a wok. However, it can rust, and must therefore be seasoned. Glass, porcelain, and ceramic do not conduct heat very well, but they do retain heat efficiently, and do not react with the foods cooked in them. It is important to remember to never subject these materials to rapid, extreme temperature changes, as they may crack easily. The best thing to do is pick the material which best suits the intended use of the particular item.

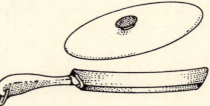

Pots & Pans Checklist:
1, 2, and 4 quart capacity Sauce Pans with lids
4 and 6 quart Casserole Dishes with tight fitting lids — Choose enameled cast iron or steel, or anodized aluminum as these can also be used on a burner.
4 individual and 1 large Gratin Baking Dishes
8 and 10 quart Stock Pots with lids
6" Omelette Pan
8" and 10" Skillets — Of a heavy metal with an oven proof handle.
10" and 12" Sauté Pans with lids — Choose those which are straight sided and flat bottomed.
12" x 18" x 2-1/2" Open Roasting Pan — In a heavy gauge metal, with a stainless steel adjustable roasting rack to fit inside of it.
1 Dutch Oven with lid — Of enameled cast iron.
14" Wok — Of iron, aluminum, or steel.
2 quart Double Boiler — Of heatproof glass.

KNIVES

Knives, your other critical tools, can also last a lifetime, as long as they are treated properly. They should be sharpened regularly, and they should never be put in the dishwasher, or allowed to soak in sudsy water. They should be rinsed with hot water and mild soap if necessary, wiped down with a clean cloth, and stored in a rack or similar set up, such that the blades won't be banging into each other or anything else. High carbon stainless steel knives are going to be your best bet, as they won't rust, and they are soft enough to sharpen properly. Also, look for knives with a full tang, where the shaft of the blade continues all the way through the handle. This will ensure that the blade will not fall away from its handle.

The three most important knives are a good French knife, also known as a chef's knife, a slicing knife, and a paring knife. The French knife has a wide, tapering triangular blade, 8" to 12" long, and should be properly weighted. It is your main knife, and will be used for cutting, slicing, julienning, and chopping. The slicing knife, 6" to 10" long, has a thin, supple blade, and is used for slicing meats. The paring knife is 3" to 6" long and is used for peeling and mincing. In addition to these basics, you will probably want to add kitchen scissors, a good cleaver and a serrated edged bread knife, and if you cook a lot of meats, a boning knife would be a good choice.

Knife Checklist:
8", 10" or 12" French Knife
6", 8" or 10" Slicing Knife
3" or 4" and 6" Paring Knives
7-1/2 " Serrated Knife
3" or 5" Boning Knife
Cleaver
Kitchen Scissors
Mortar and Pestal
Sharpening Steel or a Whetstone
Chopping Board — Wood or polyethylene, at least 18" x 18".

MACHINES

Food Processor — With dough blade, steel chopping blade,
      grating, and slicing discs. Heavy enough base that it will not
      move during operation.
Stand Mixer — With dough hook, wire balloon whisk, and
      a flat beater. Again, a good heavy base is essential.
Hand Held Mixer — Should be well balanced, easy to hold
      for short periods, and 2 to 3 pounds.
Blender — Good, solid construction, with a 3 to 4 pint capacity.

STORAGE EQUIPMENT

Nesting Rigid Containers with lids — Choose those which have
      straight sides, and are transparent.
Plastic "Ziplock" Bags
Plastic Wrap
Wax Paper
Freezer Paper
Aluminum Foil

BAKING EQUIPMENT

3 or 4 Cookie/Baking Sheets — They should be the largest
      size that fits in your oven, allowing 2" of space between
      the edges and the walls of the oven. Choose the heaviest you can
      find. It is also desirable to get the type with an upturned edge
      on one side, for ease of removal.
1 or 2 Jelly Roll Pans — The standard size is 12" x 7" x 3/4".
      Again, choose the heaviest possible.
1 or 2 Bread Pans — Of aluminum, steel, or heatproof glass, in a 9"
      x 5" x 3" size.
1   8"   Square Cake Pan — Of glass, aluminum, or tinned steel.
1   8" or 9" Round Cake Pan — Of aluminum or steel.
1   9" Springform Pan — Of the heaviest steel available,   check to
      make sure the base fits snuggly into the sides. Also look
      for one with interchangeable bottoms, including a flat bottom, a
      flat bottom with a tube, and a fluted bottom with a tube.
1   10" Tube Pan — Used to make angel food cakes, choose
      one of aluminum or steel.

BAKING EQUIPMENT — Continued
1 8-1/2" Bundt Pan — Cast aluminum with a 9 cup capacity is best.
2 9" or 10" Pie Pans — Of aluminum, steel or heatproof glass.
1 8" or 10" Quiche Pan — Get one in steel with a removeable bottom.
2 Muffin Pans — Of aluminum, steel, or cast iron with 6 or 12
     2-3/4" cups.

TERRINES & MOLDS
1 or 2 Paté Molds — Rectangular or oval fluted work best.
1 or 2 Paté Terrines with covers — Cast iron rectangular or porcelain
     oval work best.
1 Earthenware Terrine — Be sure to wash and dry this one
     by hand.
4 or 6 4 ounce Ramekins — Of porcelain, used for individual
     servings, and as sauce servers.
1, 1-1/2, 2 and 4 quart Soufflé Molds — Of porcelain, can
also be used as serving dishes.
1 8 cup Ring Mold — Also known as a rice ring, in steel,
     aluminum or glass.
3 or 4 Decorative Aspic and Gelatin Molds — Of aluminum,
     steel, copper, or earthenware.
1 or 2 Ice Cream Molds with covers — Of steel or plastic.

MEASURING EQUIPMENT
Measuring Spoons — In 1/8, 1/4, 1/2 and 1 teaspoon, and 1
     Tablespoon sizes.
Glass Liquid Measuring Cups — In 1, 2, 4, and 6 cup sizes.
Dry Measuring Cups — In 1/4, 1/3, 1/2, 1, and 2 cup sizes.
Spring or Bowl Scale — In both ounce and gram measures.
Oven Thermometer — In stainless steel, measuring from 100° to
     600°.
Meat Thermometer — In stainless steel, measuring from 0° to
     220°.
Timer — The best measures like a stopwatch from 1 second to 4
     hours.

BOWLS

3 or 4 Nesting Mixing Bowls — In stainless steel, glass, or plastic, in a range of 1-1/2 to 6-1/2 quart sizes.

2 quart Batter Bowl — In plastic or glass, with handle and spout.

10" or 12" diameter Unlined Copper Bowl — For beating egg whites.

ASSORTED & SUNDRY TOOLS

Can Opener	Bottle Opener
Wooden Spoons, various sizes	Cork Screw
Slotted or Perforated Spoon	Ladle
Large 2 Prong Fork	Poultry Shears
Metal Skewers	Baking Nails
Tongs	Large Chopsticks
Rubber Scrapers	Spatulas
Bulb Baster	Grater
Pepper Mill	Wire Whisk
Potato Ricer or Masher	Egg Beater
Garlic Press	Juicer
Vegetable Peeler	Vegetable Steamer
Vegetable Brush	Pastry Brush
Rolling Pin	Sifter
Sieve	Colander
Salad Spinner	Funnel
Pot Holders	Dish Towels

FOODSTUFFS

As long as you keep the following in your pantry and/or refrigerator, you will be able to make use of most of your leftovers with confidence.

Canned Smoked Oysters & Clams

Canned Crabmeat

Canned Bamboo Shoots

Canned Water Chestnuts

Canned Fruit

Cream of Mushroom Soup

Tomato Paste

Dried Onion Flakes

Dehydrated Potatoes

Pastas — a variety

Pudding Mixes

Pie Crust Mixes

Evaporated Milk

Ketchup

Mayonnaise

Anchovy Paste

Lemon Juice

Olive Oil

Soy Sauce

Worcestershire Sauce

Flour

Corn Starch

Honey

Jams and Jellies

Currants

Nuts

Olives

Garlic

Plain Yogurt

Heavy Cream

Canned Tuna

Canned Vegetables

Canned Mushrooms

Canned Beans

Canned Soup

Tomato Sauce

Bouillon Cubes

Onion Soup Mix

Rices — a variety

Bread Crumbs

Cake Mixes

Pie Shells

Powdered Milk

Dijon Mustard

Horseradish

Chutney

Vinegar

Vegetable Oil

Sesame Oil

Tabasco Sauce

Sugar

Gelatin

Peanut Butter

Raisins

Dried Apricots

Almonds

Potatoes

Onions

Sour Cream

Milk

Cheeses — Cheddar, Gruyere, Parmesan, Swiss, and Jack

SEASONINGS & SPICES

The following is a list of the seasonings and spices which are most often called for in recipes. Experiment with them freely, for if variety is truly the spice of life, then confidence using these tools is crucial!

Allspice — pickles, cakes, cookies, desserts
Anise Seeds — cookies, sauerkraut, coleslaw
Basil — tomatoes, fish, poultry
Bay Leaf — stews, pot roasts
Carraway Seeds — breads, rolls
Cardamon — cookies, coffees, marinades
Cayenne Pepper — sauces, meat dishes, cheese dishes
Chervil — fish, garnishes
Chili Powder — hot sauces, spicy dishes
Cinnamon — cookies, coffees
Cloves — stocks, meat pies, broths
Coriander — Mexican, Oriental and Latin American food
Cumin — Mexican dishes, chilis, stews, soups, sauces
Curry — Indian and Oriental dishes, marinades
Dill Weed — fish, poultry, lamb, veal
Fennel — fish, duck, goose, lentils
Ginger — Chinese dishes, fruits
Mace — stews, seafood, desserts
Marjoram — stuffings, lamb, spinach, zucchini, peas
Mustard — Chinese dishes, salad dressings, marinades
Nutmeg — meats, soups, puddings, desserts
Oregano — Italian dishes, stews, stuffings, tomatoes
Paprika — color, soups, stews, sauces, veal, chicken
Parsley — garnishes, stews, stocks
Pepper — everything, especially stocks, sauces, and meat
Rosemary — salmon, poultry
Sage — stuffings, pork
Salt — your most basic seasoning, but be careful to use after food is prepared, to prevent a tough texture
Sesame Seeds — breads, rolls
Thyme — stuffings, stews, soups, stocks, carrots, onions, potatoes, peas
Tarragon — soups, seafood, sauces
Tumeric — Indian dishes

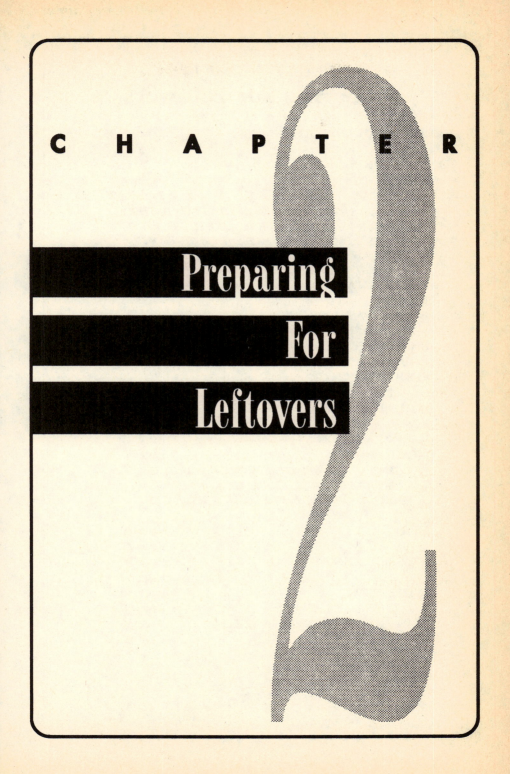

CHAPTER

Preparing
For
Leftovers

2

PLANNING FOR LEFTOVERS

In order to best utilize your leftovers, it pays off to think about how you will be using your leftovers ahead of time. For instance, when you are making your Thanksgiving turkey, you know that Friday morning is going to leave you staring at a carcass and at least a few leftover pounds of meat. So when you go to the store for your holiday shopping, pick up those "extras" that can turn your leftovers into Turkey Noodle Soup (see page 60), Jambalaya (see page 139) or Turkey Tetrazzini (see page 149). Another option is to purposefully make a little bit more than you will need, in order to get rid of other ingredients you may have around. In other words, if you have a few apples around that no one seems to be eating, make a leg of lamb one night, and turn the leftovers into Curried Lamb with Apples (see page 155). Similarly, almost any good soup, salad, or pasta sauce can be a wonderful way to use up leftover vegetables and meats.

Another key to planning for leftovers is to keep the basic items which you like to eat stored in your pantry or refrigerator (See *Basics You Should Always Have Around* — FOODSTUFFS, page 19). A classic vehicle for using up your leftovers are pasta dishes. Leftover pasta can be used in casseroles (see page 129) and can be topped with any number of sauces, hot, or cold (see page 122). Pasta can also serve as the basis for many wonderful salads. Simply add any leftover cooked vegetables, or steam those few remaining raw vegetables, toss in any cooked meats, and top it with any leftover vinaigrette (see page 117) or creme dressings (I love using Ranch style dressing on my pasta salads). Toss. Taste. Adjust the seasonings, and Enjoy!

An equally simple food dish to make use of your leftovers is to add them to quesadillas which are a Mexican dish based on the use of flour tortillas, cheese, and salsa. Simply place a flour tortilla on a baking tray, sprinkle it with grated cheese, and add any leftover cooked rice, fish, meats, vegetables, or beans. Place under the broiler until the cheese is bubbling, remove, and top with a dollop of sour cream and salsa. These can also be made in the microwave, for a quick snack.

Other dishes which can incorporate any number of different leftovers include omelettes (see page 50), crêpes (see page 107), soups (see page 59), spreads (see page 63), dressings, sauces and stuffings (see *Dressings, Sauces & Garnishes*, page 115-125), casseroles (see page 129), and soufflés (see page 85). Read the introductions to these dishes, and experiment with the leftovers you have on hand.

Remember, the most important thing to keep in mind is to experiment freely. Use the recipes in this book as a guideline, but feel free to substitute ingredients. For example, if you are interested in making manicotti, and you have leftover beef, by all means, make a beef version of our Spinach & Chicken Filled Manicotti (see page 150-151). In most cases, chicken, beef, lamb, and even fish can be substituted in different recipes. Just spice accordingly. Similarly, if you have walnuts or pecans, but no almonds, make the switch. Having sour cream but no milk or cream on hand is not a problem as in most cases, you can add some water to the sour cream to thin it down as a substitute. The trick is to get comfortable with the flavors and spices which intrigue you, and then combine what you've got, making good use of interesting texture and color combinations.

GENERAL HINTS

ARTICHOKES
Before cooking, soak in water and 1 Tablespoon of vinegar. Cook in the same mixture to tenderize leaves and keep their bright green color.

BAKING TIPS
BAKING IN GLASS AS OPPOSED TO METAL
Glass pans will brown goods faster than their metal cousins, so when using glass, you can bake goods at a slightly lower temperature for less time.

BATTER
Do not overmix waffle or muffin batters. The lumps make the baked goods fluffier. When adding fruits or nuts to batter, first coat them in flour to keep them evenly dispersed and prevent them from sinking to the bottom.

CONVERTING PLAIN FLOUR TO CAKE FLOUR
For each cup to be converted, remove 1 Tablespoon of plain flour, and replace it with 1 Tablespoon of corn starch. Then sift.

PREVENT CAKES FROM STICKING
Cut a brown paper grocery sack to fit the interior of the pan. Add the mix, bake, and peel off the liner when cake is still warm. The same applies for cupcakes.

PREVENT CRUSTS FROM STICKING
Grease pie pan with a little butter or margarine before adding crust. Pie should slide right out.

PREVENT CRUSTS FROM SOGGING
Brush crust with beaten egg white before baking, or bake crust alone for 5 or 6 minutes to firm it up. This way, the filling won't soak into the crust.

PREVENT WAFFLE IRON FROM STICKING
After using waffle iron, while it is still warm, place a piece of wax paper in between the upper and lower grids before closing and storing.

BAKED POTATOES
To speed up cooking time, par boil the potatoes for 10 minutes. Then push a metal baking nail end to end through each potato to ensure soft insides. Potato skin should then be rubbed with butter before baking, and baked for 1 hour at 400° to get skin nice and crispy.

BANANAS
If overly ripe, peel them, wrap tightly in plastic and then in foil, and freeze. Serve as a dessert, covered in chocolate.

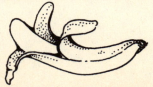

BOILING PASTA TO THE "UNSTICKING" POINT

To prevent pasta buildup, use plenty of water, approximately one gallon per pound of pasta. Once the water is boiling rapidly, add a small amount of butter or fat, and all of the pasta needed at the same time. Stir it immediately for the first minute or so, until the water returns to a boil, and the pasta is stirred by the action of the water. Incidently, do not add salt to the water beforehand, as this tends to make the pasta a bit tough.

CHOCOLATE DIPPING TIP

Make sure that whatever you are dipping is completely dry. Otherwise the moisture will get into the chocolate which will cause it to harden and become unworkable. Also, make sure that the water in the bottom section of the double boiler is simmering, not boiling. If the water gets too hot, the chocolate may become discolored.

COLOR & TEXTURE

Be aware of color — add brights to liven up your dishes. Try fresh herbs, tomatoes, bell peppers and greens. Create contrasting textures. Add crunch with celery, peppers, nuts, water chestnuts, and bacon. Do not use too many leftover ingredients in any one dish. Keep enough fresh ingredients so that the food doesn't "sag".

CONVERSIONS FOR MEASUREMENTS

3 teaspoons = 1 Tablespoon
2 Tablespoons = 1/8 cup = 1 fluid ounce
4 Tablespoons = 1/4 cup = 2 fluid ounces
5-1/3 Tablespoons = 1/3 cup = 2-2/3 fluid ounces
8 Tablespoons = 1/2 cup = 4 fluid ounces
16 Tablespoons = 1 cup = 1/2 pint = 8 fluid ounces
2 cups = 1 pint = 16 fluid ounces
4 cups = 2 pints = 1 quart
16 cups= 8 pints = 4 quarts = 1 gallon

DELUMPING GRAVIES & SAUCES

Strain lumpy gravy or sauce through a very fine sieve, and then return to heat. If sauce is now too thin, add a little cold water or stock to a couple of teaspoons of flour, mix well, and then stir into the gravy or sauce.

EGGS
ADDING EGGS TO A HOT OR HEATED SAUCE
Beat the eggs in a separate bowl first. Add a small amount of the heated sauce to the eggs, and blend rapidly. Once thoroughly mixed, add a little more sauce, stir again, and then add the egg mixture to the rest of the sauce, stirring quickly with a wire whisk.

DETERMINING IF AN EGG IS FRESH
Place the egg in a bowl of cold water. If it floats, DO NOT USE IT! A fresh egg will sink.

IDEAL EGG TEMPERATURE
It is usually best to cook eggs at room temperature. If removed from the refrigerator, run eggs under warm water before using.

METAL & EGGS
When boiling eggs or using egg yolks in sauces, one should use a pot made of glass, enameled cast iron, or anodized aluminum, as eggs cause an oxidation that tends to discolor nonanodized aluminum pans. You should also never use metal utensils near eggs, as the eggs will discolor to a greyish green. So use wooden or plastic utensils when cooking eggs.

JUICING A LEMON
Microwave the lemon for 1 minute on high, or boil in water for 10 minutes when whole. Roll under you hand, cut, and squeeze. You will get almost twice as much juice.

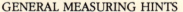

MEASURING TIPS
GENERAL MEASURING HINTS
It is best to measure liquids in glass cups, and solids in metal cups. Place the glass on an even level, the counter is usually your best bet, and look at the liquid at eye level to measure accurately. When measuring solids, choose a cup which measures the amount needed (you may have to use them in combinations), pour in the ingredient, and smoothly level the mixture to the brim of the cup with a knife or spatula.

BUTTER
1 stick = 8 Tablespoons = 1/2 cup = 4 ounces

CHEESE
4 cups grated cheese = 1 pound ungrated cheese

CHOCOLATE
1 ounce = 1 square of baking chocolate

EGGS
1 cup whole eggs = 4 to 6 whole eggs
1 cup egg whites = 8 to 10 egg whites
1 cup egg yolks = 12 to 14 egg yolks

FLOUR
4-1/2 cups sifted cake flour = 1 pound cake flour
4 cups sifted white flour = 1 pound white flour
3-1/2 cups whole wheat flour = 1 pound whole wheat flour

GELATIN
1 Tablespoon = 1/4 ounce envelope

LEGUMES
2-1/2 cups uncooked kidney beans = 1 pound uncooked beans =
    6 cups cooked beans
2-1/4 cups uncooked lentils = 1 pound uncooked lentils =
    5 cups cooked lentils
2 cups uncooked white beans = 1 pound uncooked beans =
    6 cups cooked beans

MEAT & POULTRY
4 cups cooked meat = 1 pound cooked meat

MUSHROOMS
1 to 1-1/2 cups sliced mushrooms = 1/2 pound mushrooms

NUTS
1/2 cup almond nut meats = 1 pound unshelled almonds
2-1/4 cups pecan nut meats = 1 pound unshelled pecans
2 cups walnut nut meats = 1 pound unshelled walnuts

PASTA
2 cups uncooked macaroni = 8 ounces uncooked pasta = 4 to
    4-1/2 cups cooked pasta

3-1/2 cups uncooked noodles = 8 ounces uncooked pasta = 4-1/2 cups cooked pasta

RICE
2 cups uncooked rice = 1 pound uncooked rice = 6 cups cooked rice

SUGAR
2-1/4 cups brown sugar = 1 pound brown sugar
2-1/4 cups granulated sugar = 1 pound granulated sugar
2-3/4 cups powdered sugar = 1 pound powdered sugar

MEAT
BROWNING LARGE AMOUNTS
Brown large amounts of meat in small batches. Too much meat in the skillet will lower the temperature, and meat will get watery.

JUICY BURGERS
For juicier burgers, add a little egg yolk or ice water to the ground beef before forming patties.

MARINATING TOUGH CUTS
If meat is very tough, add some strong brewed tea to the marinade, and the tannin will act as a tenderizer.

POULTRY
BROWNING THE SKIN
Rub the skin with butter or mayonnaise before baking. Or baste the skin with a mixture of butter and soy sauce a few minutes before it is finished baking.

CUTTING UP A WHOLE BIRD
Firm up the bird by first placing it in the freezer which will make it easier to cut, and be sure to use a very sharp knife when cutting.

FRYING TRICKS
After dredging in flour, chill pieces for 20 minutes before frying. This prevents the coating from falling off while frying. Then, place dark meat pieces in frying oil a few minutes before you add the white meat, as dark meat takes slightly longer to cook than white.

RICE REHEATING

When reheating, put rice in a tightly covered casserole and bake at 450° for 5 minutes, lower the oven to 350°, and continue baking for 15 to 20 minutes. Or, add a few Tablespoons of water or milk, and heat over a low flame for 4 to 5 minutes.

SALT TIP

Do not salt water before cooking beans, pasta, or corn, as they will toughen. Also, do not add salt to eggs or meat before cooking, as it draws out the juices, dries them out, and makes them tough also.

SAUTÉ TRICK

When heating butter or oil to saute food, heat the pan first, and then add the fat. That way, things are less likely to stick.

SCALDING LIQUIDS

Heat the liquid to 185°, or to the point at which it is just about to boil, but is not yet bubbling.

SEASONING & CLEANING A SKILLET

Pour a good amount of salad or cooking oil into the pan. Once on the stove, heat the pan until the oil is almost at the smoking point. Immediately remove the pan from the heat, and let it stand until the oil is cool. Once cooled, pour out the oil and wipe off the excess. If it is a cast iron skillet, place inside an oven after wiping, and a bake at a low temperature until the skillet is dry to the touch. If the skillet is to be used in dishes where a smooth surface is necessary, such as omelettes and crepes, do not scrub the surface when cleaning. The pan should be wiped out with a dish towel, and if particles are stuck to the surface, pour a little salt on the surface and rub with a towel. Do not use soap unless you plan to reseason the pan again, and if the skillet is iron, it must be dried immediately, or it will rust.

STOCKS
CLEARING A STOCK
Beat an egg white, along with its shell, in a few teaspoons of cold water. Pour the mixture into the stock, boil for a few minutes, and then strain the stock.

DE FATTING A STOCK
Float ice cubes or lettuce leaves over the top of the stock, and the fat will cling to them.

STOCK SUBSTITUTIONS
When stock is called for in a recipe, in a pinch, you can substitute the bouillon of whatever is called for, ie: vegetable, fish, poultry, or meat. Just dissolve the bouillon in the same amount of hot water as the amount of stock called for in the recipe.

THINGS TO COME IN...

Preparing For Leftovers

STORAGE TECHNIQUES

The storage equipment list from *Basics You Should Always Have Around* is discussed here in greater detail. The storage information which follows the equipment explanation will help you efficiently utilize all of your food purchases. The storage techniques are divided according to food group categories.

EQUIPMENT

NESTING RIGID CONTAINERS WITH LIDS
Straight sided containers stack, pack, and unpack better, and take up less space. Transparency means you can see what you've got, and you will be more likely to use your leftovers. However, some things, like dried foods, herbs and spices, and staples need protection from light, so keep them in opaque containers. Also, you should have a wide variety of sizes, because there should be very little air space left once the container is filled.

PLASTIC "ZIPLOCK" BAGS
The sturdier ones are useful for freezing leftovers. Fill, and squeeze out any extra air before sealing in order to keep foods fresher, longer.

PLASTIC WRAP
Heavier wraps like Saran Wrap work the best in the freezer, as they cling the tightest. However, if you are going to use plastic wrap in the microwave, do not use Saran Wrap or anything made with polyvinyl chloride, as it has been found to leach chemicals into the food when it is cooked. In this case, the best plastic wrap to use is Handi-Wrap II or Glad Cling Wrap.

WAX PAPER
Inexpensive, and a useful tool in baking, it is not a very effective way to store many foods other than raw meat or bread.

FREEZER PAPER

Although it does not mold as well as plastic wrap or foil, it can be purchased in 18" widths, so oftentimes it is the best option. When used for freezing, it should be lined with plastic, not wax, and must be taped with freezer tape. Use the following folding technique to seal out air: Cut a piece of paper that is twice as long and wide as whatever you are wrapping. Place food in the center of the paper. Pull up two opposing edges until they meet in the center above the food. Turn the edges down together and crease at 1/4". Continue to fold these over onto themselves, creasing every 1/4" as you go, until it folds flat on top of the food. Tape this fold down. Then, on each open side, press the paper flat, and fold the corners in to form a "V" shape. Fold the point of the "V" up, and flatten against the side of the food, taping the sides up.

ALUMINUM FOIL

The heaviest weights can be used for freezing. Its stiffness makes it useful for protecting fragile goods, like pie crusts, and it can conform to an almost airtight seal on any size or shape container. The fold described above for freezer paper is the best way to keep air out, and the tape is unnecessary. When storing acidic or salty foods, or those made with alcohol, it is important to remember that aluminum foil will get "pits" from such ingredients due to electrolytic or chemical action. While this pitting is not harmful or toxic, it is best to scrape away the pitting before eating. For aesthetic purposes, you might want to wrap these items in plastic wrap first, and then wrap them in foil.

TECHNIQUES

GRAINS, PASTAS, CEREALS & STAPLES
Grains, pastas, cereals, and staples of all kinds must be kept away from moisture, humidity, sunlight, and bugs. Thus, they should be stored in airtight plastic bags or lidded containers in a cool, dry, dark place. Fresh made pasta should be stored in a plastic bag in the refrigerator. Leftovers should be coated in oil or butter, and stored in a tightly lidded container or sealed plastic bag in the refrigerator.

NUTS & SEEDS
If purchased in their shells, nuts and seeds should be free from holes and cracks. If shelled, they should be free from mold, as nut meat mold can be highly toxic. They should look plump and full, and should be of uniform color. They should be stored in airtight containers away from direct sunlight. Storing them in the pantry, refrigerator, or freezer is fine.

BAKED GOODS
BREADS
Soft crusted breads should be tightly wrapped in a plastic bag, and refrigerated. Hard crusted breads should be stored loosely in wax paper or a paper bag at room temperature.

CAKES
Store in an airtight plastic bag or container in a cool, dry place like a pantry or cupboard.

COOKIES
Soft cookies should be stored in a container with a tight fitting lid. Crisper cookies are fine with a loose fitting lid. However, do not store together, as both textures will lose out. To store cookie dough, pour batter into an old juice can, wrap tightly, and freeze. To bake frozen dough, thaw for 15 minutes, push out of can, slice thin, and bake.

CRACKERS
Seal in an airtight plastic bag or canister, and store in a cool, dry place like a pantry or cupboard.

PASTRIES
Wrap tightly in plastic, and refrigerate.

PIES
Store loosely covered with plastic or foil in the fridge.

DAIRY PRODUCTS
Almost without exception, all dairy products should be kept in the refrigerator in their original packages or in tightly sealed containers. Be sure to check freshness dates on a regular basis, and purchase products well before this date, so that they will be useable longer.

BUTTER & MARGARINE
Keep any unwrapped sticks in a covered container or on a covered dish, as butter and margarine are particularly succeptible to absorbing other odors.

CHEESES
Carefully slice off any unwanted mold, wrap cheeses tightly in plastic, and refrigerate. Feta cheese should be placed in a container and soaked in a salt water brine or milk. Cover it tightly, and refrigerate it.

EGGS
You should keep eggs in the refrigerator. Yolks can be stored in the refrigerator in a shallow bowl, covered with cold water. Whites should be kept in the refrigerator in a tightly covered container. Both the whites and the yolks will freeze nicely. You can store many in a well sealed plastic container in the freezer. You may prefer to store them singly when accuracy is critical to a recipe. In this case, put each yolk and/or white in an individual compartment in an ice tray. Pop out the frozen product, and wrap tightly in plastic wrap.

ICE CREAM
Store in original container in the freezer. To prevent freezer burn and drying out once opened, place a layer of plastic wrap over the surface of the unused ice cream, seal the carton in a plastic bag, and return to the freezer.

FISH
Fresh fish should be dried, wrapped tightly in plastic or foil, then sealed airtight in a plastic bag and refrigerated. If storing in the refrigerator for longer than 1 full day, you should coat the fish with soy sauce or salt water before wrapping. Do not freeze fresh fish. Smoked fish should be wrapped tightly in plastic and refrigerated. Canned and dried fish should be kept in a cool, dry location. Once opened, transfer it to a tightly lidded glass or plastic container, and refrigerate. Any leftover cooked fish should be wrapped tightly in plastic and refrigerated.

CLAMS, MUSSELS, OYSTERS & SCALLOPS
Store fresh, live shellfish in saltwater in a shallow pan, and cover them with a wet cloth. BE SURE TO ONLY COOK ANIMALS WHICH ARE STILL ALIVE! Cooked shellfish should be wrapped tightly and stored in the refrigerator.

CRABS, CRAYFISH & LOBSTERS
Live animals should be packed by the sales person in seaweed in a special crate, and may be kept refrigerated for a few days. BE SURE TO ONLY COOK ANIMALS WHICH ARE STILL ALIVE! Cooked shellfish should be wrapped tightly and stored in the refrigerator.

SHRIMP
Store fresh shrimp on a bed of ice in the refrigerator. Cooked shrimp should be sealed airtight in a plastic bag, and refrigerated.

MEAT & POULTRY

Fresh meat and poultry should be stored wrapped, but with enough circulation to dry their surfaces of excess moisture, in the coldest part of the refrigerator. The film on packaged meats and poultry is usually permeable, so you can leave these in their original packages. You can also rinse the meat or poultry, pat dry, and wrap loosely in wax paper, plastic, or foil. Leaky packages should be kept away from other food, either in a separate compartment, or on a plate. Be careful to keep your refrigerator washed of such juices, as they are a common reason for bacterial growth. Refrigerated raw meat should be cooked within 2 or 3 days as it will otherwise spoil. Thus, freezing is often the best storage technique for meat and poultry. When freezing, follow the instructions given in the equipment section under FREEZER PAPER, page 34. Before freezing, remove all bones, and save bones and scraps in a sealed plastic bag in the freezer for use in stocks and other recipes. Be sure to fully thaw frozen meat and poultry before using. Once meat or poultry has been cooked, leftovers should be wrapped immediately, while still warm. Wrap leftovers tightly in plastic or foil, or place in a tightly covered container, and refrigerate.

VEGETABLES

When purchasing vegetables, you should always buy the freshest available and buy frequently as opposed to buying too many at once. This way you won't be "stuck" with too many emergency leftover dishes to concoct at once. Look for firm vegetables, and bright, deep colors, avoiding those that are damaged, as they will spoil faster. For the most part, vegetables should be stored at high humidity, and low temperatures. Thus, the best place to store most vegetables is in your refrigerator. Most refrigerators have a separate drawer, called a vegetable crisper, and this is the ideal location for raw vegetables. They should be stored unwashed, and dry to the touch in plastic bags. Be sure to dry vegetables thoroughly, as moisture on the vegetable will promote the growth of bacteria. To keep them fresh as long as possible, do not wash or cut them until you are ready to use them. In general, it is a good idea to store vegetables away from fruits, as the gases emitted by fresh fruit tend to change the flavors and storage length of the vegetables. Leftover cooked vegetables should be kept tightly sealed in a container in the refrigerator, or may also be frozen by placing them in a tightly sealed plastic bag or container, and placing them in the freezer. For the most part, however, frozen cooked vegetables should be added to other dishes, and not used as a dish by themselves, as their texture is altered when frozen. Storage techniques for veggies which have rules differing from those above, follow.

AVOCADOS
To prevent browning once cut, sprinkle the avocado liberally with lemon juice. To store excess avocado, mash it, mix with lemon juice, and freeze in tightly covered containers. Guacamole dip should be stored in the refrigerator covered with plastic wrap, with the avocado pit set into the top of the mixture.

CANNED VEGETABLES
Canned vegetables usually have a high sodium content, so beware. Choose cans that are in good physical condition, and store them in your pantry or a cupboard. Once opened, remove vegetables from cans and store them in glass or plastic containers, as they will otherwise take on the metal flavor of the can.

DRIED LEGUMES & VEGETABLES
These may be stored in the pantry, sealed in a plastic bag to keep out bugs and humidity. Many also make a pretty counter display when placed in decorative glass jars.

FROZEN VEGETABLES
These are usually preferable to canned, as they are fresh frozen, with no added chemicals. Choose packages where the vegetables are hard still, as they lose their texture and flavor if they have softened. Store below 0° at all times.

LETTUCES
All lettuces should be stored unwashed in a sealed bag in the crisper of the refrigerator. However, do not place lettuces near fresh fruits, as this will cause the lettuce leaves to brown. Once lettuces have been cut and washed, place in a plastic bag, fill it with air, and seal it. Then store in the refrigerator.

MUSHROOMS
Remove any plastic wrap, and refrigerate immediately in a porous box or bag, covered with a damp paper towel. When using mushrooms, never wash or peel them, unless they are brown. Merely wipe them with a dish towel or scrub them with a commercially available mushroom brush to remove any signs of dirt.

ONIONS

Remove them from the bag in which they are purchased in order to let air circulate around them. Remove any damaged items, and store them in a cool, ventilated location. Do not store next to potatoes as they each give off gases which shorten the life span of the other. Cut onions should be tightly wrapped and stored in the refrigerator.

PEPPERS

Place them in a porous paper bag — a small grocery sack will do. Seal it loosely, and keep it in the refrigerator. Or, dice them and freeze in plastic bags.

POTATOES, SWEET POTATOES & YAMS

Do not store in the refrigerator. Instead, keep them in a cool, dark, place with adequate air circulation, like in a paper bag or basket in a pantry or cupboard. Just in case they sprout, use the sprouted potatoes in baked dishes, as the prolonged exposure to heat will get rid of any potential health risks. Again, do not store near onions, as each impairs the length of storage for the other.

RUTABEGAS & TURNIPS

Cooked leftover rutabegas and turnips can be puréed and frozen in a tighly sealed container or plastic bag.

TOFU

Tofu should be stored in the refrigerator in a container full of enough water to fully cover it. The water should be replaced daily.

TOMATOES

Keep them in a cool, dark place, like in a paper bag in a pantry or cupboard. Tomatoes should be kept at room temperature until they are ripe, at which time they may be placed in the refrigerator, but you should take them out of the refrigerator and let them sit before eating so they can return to room temperature.

TOMATO PASTE
Unless you buy tomato paste in a resealable squeeze tube, you will invariably wind up with a full can less a few teaspoons. Storage is important because leaving the can, even covered, in the refrigerator, will soon yield a vibrant but inedible fuzz. Here are some tips:

1. Spread a layer of vegetable oil over the smoothed over, unused portion, and refrigerate. This should seal air out. When needed, tip the can to let the oil flow to the side, and scoop out what you need.
2. Cover the can with plastic wrap held securely with a rubber band, then freeze. When you need to use paste, open the bottom end of the can, and use it as a base to push up the frozen paste. In a small can, 1 Tablespoon is the equivalent of approximately 3/4" of the frozen paste cyclinder. Slice what you need, refreeze the rest, and use in the same manner until the paste is gone.
3. Fill ice trays by spooning paste into compartments. Fill with 1 Tablespoon and with 1 teaspoon quantities. Pop out once frozen, wrap in plastic, label sizes, and freeze until needed.

FRUITS
When purchasing fruit, try to buy those which have begun to ripen. They should be firm to the touch, have a faint sweet smell, and be free from bruises, breaks in the skin, and mold. When purchasing prepackaged fruit, be sure to open the package and pick out any damaged items before storing them, as mold tends to be contagious, and easily will pass from one item to another. For the most part, fruit should be washed and thoroughly dried before storing, as this should remove most of the residues from any pesticides still on the skin. The exceptions to this are cherries and berries, as the water is liable to soak into them and cause them to rot faster. Any wax on the skin, particularly on apples and citrus fruits, can be scrubbed off with a vegetable brush and some warm soapy water. In general, fruit should be stored at room temperature until it is ripe, at which point it should be placed in the refrigerator in a plastic bag away from vegetables, as the gases they emit tend to change the taste and hasten the decaying process of vegetables. If you would like to speed up the ripening process, take a paper bag and poke a number of small holes in it. Then place the fruit loosely in the bag, and set it in a cool, dry place. Check the bag daily and remove ripe pieces regularly. Any unused fresh fruit, if cut, should be sprinkled with lemon juice to prevent browning, wrapped tightly in plastic, and placed in the refrigerator. Fruits with different storage guidelines follow.

BLACKBERRIES & RASPBERRIES
Remove from their original cartons and pick out the moldy and bruised berries. Store them unwashed in a shallow, uncovered, container in a single layer, in order to prevent them from crushing.

BLUEBERRIES
Store them unwashed in the refrigerator, in their original carton, covered with plastic wrap.

DRIED FRUIT
Seal in a plastic bag or tightly lidded container, and store in the refrigerator. If dried fruit becomes hard, you can steam it, poach it, or soak it in any liquid in order to revive it.

JAMS, JELLIES & PRESERVES
Store unopened containers in a cool, dry, dark place such as a pantry or cupboard. Refrigerate them once they are opened.

LEMONS
Do not need to be left out to ripen first. Keep them in a plastic bag in the refrigerator.

POMEGRANATES
Cut the pomegranate open and remove the seeds to a tightly sealed container, being careful to remove all of the bitter yellow membrane. Store in the refrigerator.

STRAWBERRIES
Do not wash before storing. Remove any bruised or moldy berries, place back in original basket, and cover in plastic. Store in the refrigerator. When you do wash them, be sure to wash them with the stems on, as water will seep into the fruit otherwise.

HERBS, SEASONINGS & SPICES
Dried herbs, spices, and seasonings should be kept in a cool, dark place. You can tell if the spices are losing their strength, as their color and scent will dissipate with age. Red spices will lose their bright color, as will green herbs. Green spices will eventually turn brown. As soon as you notice a loss of color or pungency, for the sake of your gourmet fare, bid them farewell. Fresh herbs should be rinsed, patted dry, and stored in airtight jars in the refrigerator, or you can set them in a jar, with their stems fully emersed in water, in the refrigerator.

Instructions on the best way to store garlic and ginger follows.

GARLIC & GINGER
Whenever possible, use the freshest garlic and ginger you can find, as the aroma and taste far surpass those of their powdered relatives. However, storing them well is key to their not drying up. Here are a few suggestions:

1. Keep ginger root in a plastic bag in the freezer. When you need to use it, rinse it in hot water to loosen the skin, peel as much as necessary, and slice or grate as needed.

2. Grate the whole ginger root and add to a blend of equal parts water and white vinegar or sherry. Add just enough to moisten it, and keep it in a small, tightly sealed jar in the refrigerator where it can stay fresh for months. For garlic, crush a bulbs' worth of cloves, and add to a blend of equal parts water and olive oil.

3. Peel the ginger root and pour dry sherry over it. Store in a tightly sealed jar in the refrigerator.

GARLIC

CHAPTER

The
Morning
After

THINGS TO COME IN...
The Morning After

BLUE CHEESE & TOMATO TART

For Crust:
pastry for 10" pie crust
1 egg yolk, lightly beaten

For Filling:
2 Tablespoons shallots, minced
2 medium tomatoes, peeled, thinly sliced and drained
2 cups sharp blue cheese, crumbled
3 eggs, lightly beaten
2 cups heavy cream
salt & pepper to taste

To Prepare Crust:
Preheat oven to 425°. Fit pastry into a 10" tart pan with a removeable bottom. Line the pastry crust with parchment or foil and weight it down with raw rice or beans. Bake the crust at 425° for 14 to16 minutes. Remove paper and beans and brush the crust with the beaten egg yolk. Return to the oven for 2 minutes. Allow the crust to cool.

To Make Filling:
Reduce the oven temperature to 375°. Sprinkle the bottom of the crust with shallots and cover evenly with tomato slices. Distribute cheese evenly over tomato slices. Combine eggs, cream, salt and pepper and pour over tomatoes and cheese. Bake at 375° for 35 to 40 minutes until puffed and lightly browned. Note: The amount of salt used should be guided by the sharpness of the cheese.

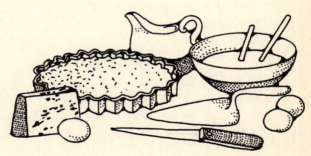

BROCCOLI QUICHE

1 prepared 9" pie crust
2 Tablespoons sweet butter
1 leek (white part only), sliced
1 cup cooked broccoli, coarsely chopped
salt & pepper to taste
1 cup Swiss cheese, grated
1/4 cup parmesan cheese, grated
3 eggs
1 cup heavy cream
1/2 cup light cream

Preheat oven to 350°. Melt 1 Tablespoon sweet butter in pan, and sauté leek until soft and limp but not brown. Combine broccoli with leek and season with salt and pepper. Line bottom of tart crust with broccoli and leek. Cover with cheeses. Combine eggs and cream and pour over vegetables and cheeses. Cut remaining Tablespoon of sweet butter into small pieces and dot top of quiche. Bake at 350° for 45 minutes or until puffed and brown. Grate parmesan cheese and grind black pepper over the quiche.

SMOKED SALMON QUICHE

1 prepared 9" pie crust
1 Tablespoon butter
1 leek (white & green parts), sliced into thin rounds
1/2 cup smoked salmon, cut into small pieces
2 Tablespoons fresh dill, chopped
3 oz. Swiss cheese, cut in small pieces
2 Tablespoons parmesan cheese, grated
2 eggs, lightly beaten
1 cup heavy cream
pepper to taste

Preheat oven to 350°. Melt butter in pan, and sauté leeks until limp. Spread leeks evenly over the bottom of the pie crust and cover with salmon. Sprinkle dill evenly over that. Distribute the cheeses evenly over the pie. Mix egg, cream, and pepper, and pour over the pie. Bake at 350° for 35 to 45 minutes until puffed and golden.

CHICKEN & MUSHROOM QUICHE

pastry for 9" crust, partially baked
2 Tablespoon butter
1 Tablespoon onion, finely chopped
1 cup mushrooms, thinly sliced
1 cup cooked chicken, diced
1/4 cup parmesan cheese, grated
6 oz. Swiss cheese, coarsely grated
4 eggs, lightly beaten
1-1/2 cups creme fraiche
1/4 teaspoon tarragon
1/2 teaspoon salt
1/4 teaspoon white pepper
2 Tablespoons parsley, chopped

Preheat oven to 450°. In a skillet, heat the butter, add the onion and mushrooms and cook until the onion is transparent. Combine the mixture with the chicken and the cheeses and distribute over the partially baked pie crust. Combine the eggs, creme fraiche, tarragon, salt, pepper, and parsley. Pour the egg mixture over the chicken mixture. Bake for 15 minutes at 450°. Reduce the oven to 350° and bake about 15 minutes more or until a knife inserted 1" from the pastry edge comes out clean. Serve immediately. Steamed green beans sprinkled with parmesan go well with quiche, both for texture and color. Add a side dish of sliced tomatoes drizzled with olive oil and cover with fresh chopped or dried basil.

OMELETTES

The omelette is a truly delicious dish that depends upon the usage of small amounts of precooked and leftover foods for much of its existence. Where else could only 2 Tablespoons of crabmeat have such significance? Almost any leftover can be incorporated into an omelette — herbs, cheese, vegetables, fish, poultry or meats. Just use whatever you have on hand.

BASIC OMELETTE

1 Tablespoon water
1/4 teaspoon salt
2 eggs
1-1/2 teaspoons butter

Add water and salt to eggs, and beat well. Melt the butter in a heavy 6" or 8" iron skillet. The butter should be bubbly hot but not smoking or brown. Pour the egg mixture into the skillet and start loosening the edges of the mixture with a spatula, lifting up the eggs where they have set, and let the uncooked part run underneath.

When the omelette is set, pour the sauce or filling (use approximately 1/3 cup of filling for each omelette) on the top and fold over into the omelette as you roll it onto the platter. An alternate method for omelette making is to mix bits of leftover foods directly into the basic omelette recipe, and then cook as directed above.

Fillings for omelettes are limitless. Some standard ones are:

1. Grated cheese, chopped scallions, and herbs
2. Creamed chicken or turkey
3. Creamed shrimp or crabmeat flavored with dill
4. Creamed mushrooms
5. Leftover vegetables, cooked and diced
6. Leftover ratatouille
7. Leftover caviar (if you are that lucky) & sour cream

CURRIED MUSHROOM OMELETTE

1-1/2 teaspoons butter
1/4 teaspoon curry powder
1/4 cup mushrooms, chopped
1 shallot, minced
1 basic omelette recipe (see page 50)

Melt butter in skillet and add curry powder. Sauté mushrooms and shallots in the curry butter. Make a basic omelette and fill with the mushrooms.

CRABMEAT OMELETTE

1-1/2 teaspoons butter
2 Tablespoons cooked crabmeat
2 Tablespoons onion, chopped
2 Tablespoons tomato, chopped
2 Tablespoons green pepper, chopped
1 basic omelette recipe (see page 50)

Melt butter in a skillet over moderate heat, and sauté the crabmeat, onion, tomato, and pepper. Make a basic omelette and fill with the crabmeat mixture.

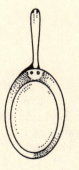

SMOKED SALMON OMELETTE

2 Tablespoons smoked salmon, finely
    chopped
1-1/2 teaspoons capers, drained and minced
1-1/2 teaspoons heavy cream
1 teaspoon lemon juice
1 basic omelette recipe (see page 50),
    without the water

Mix ingredients with the basic omelette recipe omitting the water. Cook according to the basic omelette instructions.

SALAMI & CHEESE OMELETTE

1 teaspoon butter
2 Tablespoons salami, finely minced
1 Tablespoon green onion, finely minced
1 Tablespoon gruyere cheese, grated
1 basic omelette recipe (see page 50)

Sauté salami and green onion in butter for 1 or 2 minutes. Reserve and mix with cheese. Make a basic omelette and fill with salami mixture.

DENVER OMELETTE

1-1/2 teaspoons butter
1 Tablespoon green pepper, minced
1 Tablespoon onion, minced
2 Tablespoons cooked ham, minced
1 basic omelette recipe (see page 50)

Sauté the pepper, onion and ham in the butter. Make a basic omelette and fill with ham mixture.

PANAMA EGGS

2 Tablespoons butter
1 onion, finely diced
2 cups sharp cheddar cheese, grated
1 tomato, diced and drained
6 eggs, lightly beaten

Heat heavy iron frying pan and melt butter (do not brown). Sauté onion in the butter. Lower heat, and stirring constantly, add cheese. Cook over low heat until cheese is thoroughly melted. Add tomato and stir to coat tomato with cheese. Add eggs and gently mix from the bottom of pan. Cook only until eggs are set, as overcooking will result in a rubbery texture. Put eggs in a heated serving bowl and serve at once.

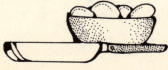

FRENCH TOAST

2 eggs, beaten lightly
1 cup heavy cream, light cream
    or milk
1/3 cup sugar
1 teaspoon vanilla
6 slices of bread, crusts trimmed
    if desired
powdered sugar

In a large bowl, add eggs and cream or milk, and beat. Add sugar and vanilla. Dip bread into egg mixture. Turn bread over and coat both sides completely. Heat on a greased, preheated griddle or frying pan until golden brown on both sides. Sprinkle with powdered sugar and serve with jam.

RICH FRENCH TOAST

1 cup eggnog
2 eggs, lightly beaten
1 teaspoon vanilla
1/3 cup sugar
1/4 teaspoon nutmeg
6 slices of stale bread, 1/2" thick,
    crusts removed
2 Tablespoons sweet butter
confectioner's sugar

Combine eggnog, eggs, vanilla, sugar and nutmeg, and mix well. Place bread slices in a shallow rectangular baking dish and pour the eggnog mixture over it. Soak bread slices for about 10 minutes or until soft, turning frequently. Grill toast on a greased, preheated medium high griddle. Turn slices when they are golden brown on the underside. Top each slice with 1 teaspoon of sweet butter and continue cooking until underside is brown. Place French toast, unbuttered side up, on a heated serving plate. Sprinkle with confectioner's sugar.

APPLE PANCAKES

2 cups flour
2 Tablespoons sugar
1 Tablespoon baking powder
1 teaspoon cinnamon
1-1/2 cups milk
2 eggs, lightly beaten
1/4 cup butter, melted
1 apple, peeled, cored and grated
1/4 cup pecans, chopped

Sift the flour, sugar, baking powder, and cinnamon together. Add the milk to the eggs and beat lightly. Combine the two mixtures and add the melted butter, apple, and pecans. Blend thoroughly. DO NOT OVERMIX. Heat a griddle over moderate heat until a few drops of cold water bounce and sputter. Grease the griddle lightly with butter. Drop the pancake batter from a 1/4 cup measure with a spout. Cook until bubbles appear on the surface. Turn pancakes and cook on the other side for about 1 minute. Serve with melted butter and honey.

APPLE MUFFINS

2 cups sifted flour
3/4 cup sugar
1 Tablespoon baking powder
2 teaspoons cinnamon
1 apple, grated
1/2 cup golden raisins
1/2 cup walnuts, chopped
1/2 cup milk
1/2 cup butter, melted
2 eggs, lightly beaten
cinnamon sugar

Preheat oven to 400°. Grease several muffin tins with butter or margarine. Sift flour, sugar, baking powder, and cinnamon into a mixing bowl. Stir in the apple, raisins, and nuts. In another bowl, mix milk, melted butter, and eggs. Make a well in the flour mixture and add the egg mixture. Mix briefly, only until the dry ingredients are combined. Spoon mixture into prepared muffin tins and sprinkle cinnamon sugar generously over the tops of the muffins. Bake at 400° for 25 to 30 minutes.

BRAN MUFFINS

1 cup bran cereal
1 cup sour milk
1 egg
1/4 cup sweet butter, melted
1/2 cup golden raisins
1-1/4 cups all purpose flour
3 teaspoons baking powder
1/2 teaspoon salt
1/2 cup sugar

Preheat oven to 400°. Grease 12 2-1/2" muffin pan cups with butter or margarine. Combine cereal and milk in a mixing bowl, mixing well. Add egg and sweet butter, and beat well. Stir in raisins. Sift together flour, baking powder, salt, and sugar. Add sifted dry ingredients to cereal mixture stirring only until combined. DO NOT OVERMIX. Divide batter into prepared muffin pan cups. Bake at 400° for 25 minutes or until golden brown.

CHAPTER

Soups
& Starters

4

THINGS TO COME IN...
Soups & Starters

SOUPS

Soup can be a delicate introduction to a meal, a base for a sauce, or a hearty meal unto itself. The foundation of any good soup is a stock, usually made from bones. Thus, when buying meat, always ask the butcher to give you the bones he may have trimmed away, and store them in the freezer. Cooked bones may also be added to your stash. A rich stock is best made by first browning bones, and then simmering them for an hour or so with vegetables, until you are left with a thick sauce. It is also possible to make stock by adding bouillon to boiling water, and then adding vegetables and simmering. In any case, soup is a wonderful vehicle for leftover fresh vegetables and fresh or cooked meats. Simply start with a stock, add whatever sounds exciting, season to taste, and simmer.

BASIC BROTH OR SOUP MADE FROM BONES

2 pounds of leftover bones from beef, veal or lamb
1 large onion studded with 5 whole cloves
4 whole carrots, scrubbed
4 celery ribs
3 parsnips
1 or 2 leeks
8 parsley sprigs
1 bay leaf
2 teaspoons tomato paste
2 cloves garlic

In a 450° oven, cook the bones in a large roasting pan until they are browned. Remove and place them in a large kettle. Cover the bones with cold water and bring to a boil. Skim off the scum as it rises to the surface. Add the rest of the ingredients, lower the heat, cover, and simmer for 2 to 3 hours. Skim frequently in the first 45 minutes. Taste. If the broth does not seem strong enough, cook uncovered for an extra 30 minutes. Strain through a sieve lined with several layers of damp cheesecloth. DO NOT SEASON until you use the broth. Refrigerate at once. (Continued on next page.)

BROTH OR SOUP FROM BONES — Continued

The fat can be easily removed when broth is chilled. If you are not planning to use it right away, store in pint sized containers in the freezer. To continue on and make a complete soup, add a cup of barley and simmer for 45 minutes. Add any vegetables that you have on hand, judging the cooking time by the type of vegetable and adding them in stages.

TURKEY NOODLE SOUP

For Broth:
1 turkey carcass (10-12 lb. bird) with some meat left on
1 large onion studded with 4 whole cloves
1 parsnip, cut in quarters
2 carrots, halved
2 celery stalks with leaves, halved
4 cloves garlic
1/2 cup fresh dill
1/4 cup parsley
4 peppercorns
salt to taste

For Soup:
2 cups egg noodles
3 carrots, peeled and cut into 1/4" rounds
1 parsnip, peeled and diced
2 celery stalks, diced
1 leek (white part only), diced
3 Tablespoons fresh dill
3 Tablespoons fresh parsley
salt & pepper to taste

Cut up carcass and place in stock pot. Add the rest of the broth ingredients to the pot, cover with cold water, and bring to a boil. Immediately reduce heat and simmer for 1-1/2 hours, with pot lid slightly ajar. Strain the broth. Reserve the turkey meat and discard the vegetables and herbs. Allow to cool. Once cooled, skim off the fat and return to heat. Bring to a boil. Add noodles and cook for 5 minutes. Add carrots and parsnips when boiling. Cook for 5 minutes. Turn heat down to a simmer, add celery and leek, and simmer for 15 minutes. Add turkey, dill, parsley, salt, and pepper to taste. Simmer 5 more minutes. Garnish with fresh parsley, and serve hot with a good crusty French bread.

ROMAINE RICE SOUP

3 Tablespoons butter
1-1/2 medium onions, finely chopped
6 cups Romaine lettuce
6 cups chicken stock
1 cup cooked rice
salt & pepper to taste
parmesan cheese, freshly grated

Melt butter in a heavy sauce pan and add onion. Cook until the onion is transparent and wilted, about 5 minutes. Add lettuce, cover and cook for 5 minutes over low heat. Add 1 cup of stock, bring to a boil and simmer for 5 minutes over low heat. Add remaining stock, rice, salt, and pepper. Simmer for 5 minutes. Before serving, sprinkle 2 teaspoons of grated parmesan over each bowl of soup. Serve with a hearty rye bread.

WHITE BEAN SOUP

2 cups (1 lb.) dried white navy beans
1 medium onion, chopped
1 meaty ham bone
1 bay leaf
salt & pepper to taste
3 parsnips, chopped

Rinse the beans and pick over to remove all foreign particles. Place the beans in a large kettle, cover with water, and let stand overnight. In a heavy pan, saute onion with fat cut from ham bone. Sear the ham bone in the same pan. Add onions and ham bone to beans and water along with the bay leaf, salt, and pepper. Cover and bring slowly to a boil. Reduce the heat, skim foam from the top, and simmer gently for 1-1/2 hours. Add the parsnips and continue to cook for 30 minutes. Remove the ham bone and shred the meat. Set meat aside. Discard the bay leaf. Puree the soup in a blender or press the vegetables through a sieve. Return the soup to the pot and add the meat. Adjust the seasonings. Rye or pumpernickle croutons as a garnish are a good dark contrast to the light colored soup.

FAUX GAZPACHO

leftover dressed green salad, with croutons removed
V-8 or tomato based juice
salt & pepper to taste

Process salad and juice in the workbowl of a food processor or purée in a blender, adding juice until desired consistency is achieved. Season to taste. Serve hot or chilled, with fresh croutons, and a dollop of sour cream or plain yogurt on top.

SPREADS

For a good spread, you need 2 basic components, a flavoring, and a binding agent. Flavorings include herbs and seasonings, dried soup mixes, vegetables, meats, poultry or fish. Some good binders are sour cream, plain yogurt, cream cheese, or any other soft cheese. The beauty of spreads is that they are so easy to make. Simply process the ingredients in the work bowl of a food processor. This leaves time for the most important aspect of a spread — its presentation. They should be served chilled, for the most part, on a platter or in a decorative mold or bowl, and surrounded by fresh vegetables or good breads and crackers.

PESTO/VEGETABLE CREAM CHEESE SPREAD

1/2 cup cream cheese
1/3 cup pesto sauce or cooked vegetables, pureed

Blend cream cheese until it is spreadable. Starting with the cream cheese, and spreading until smooth, alternate layers of cheese and pesto or puree in a small mold (a flower pot works well for this) lined with cheesecloth. Chill for 30 minutes. Invert on a chilled serving plate, and serve with crackers or fresh chopped vegetables.

NOVA SCOTIA SPREAD

any leftover smoked salmon or lox
1/2 cup cream cheese
1/4 teaspoon chives, chopped
1/4 teaspoon dill, chopped

Process all of the ingredients in the workbowl of a food processor or purée in a blender. Use as a spread on black bread or bagels. Thinned down with some heavy cream or sour cream it becomes a good sauce for omelettes.

ANCHOVY CHEESE

1 green or red bell pepper
6 oz. cream cheese
3 Tablespoons sweet butter, softened
2 anchovies, minced
1-1/2 Tablespoons onion, grated
1-1/2 teaspoons capers
1/2 teaspoon caraway seeds
3/4 teaspoon paprika (Hungarian if possible)
2 drops worcestershire sauce
salt & pepper to taste

Remove seeds and membranes from the pepper. Remove top of
pepper and reserve. Combine the other ingredients in the workbowl
of a food processor. Mix until smooth. Pack cheese mixture into the
pepper. Put top of pepper on and refrigerate. To serve, cut pepper
into horizontal rounds and serve with black bread.

CHICKEN MOUSSE

4 cups cooked chicken
1 chicken liver
1 clove garlic
4 Tablespoons butter, melted
1 cup light cream

Preheat oven to 350°. Grease a 4 cup, straight sided, shallow mold
with butter or margarine. Combine all ingredients in a blender or food
processor and process until smooth and thoroughly blended. Pour
into the prepared mold. Put mold in a baking pan and add hot water
to 1/2 the depth of the mold. Bake at 350° for 45 to 60 minutes, or
until edges leave the side of the mold and mousse colors slightly.
Allow mousse to stand for 5 minutes and then unmold on a serving
platter. Serve with sour cream dill sauce.

CHOPPED CHICKEN LIVERS

4 chicken livers
2-1/2 Tablespoons chicken fat
1/2 small onion, chopped
2 hardboiled eggs
salt & pepper to taste

Pat the chicken livers dry. Cut them in half. Melt the chicken fat in a heavy skillet over moderate heat, add the onions, and sauté until translucent. Add the chicken livers and cook until "just done". Empty the contents of the skillet into the workbowl of the food processor fitted with the steel blade. Blend until smooth. Add in the eggs and chop, turning the machine on and off. Season to taste with salt and freshly ground pepper. Add more chicken fat if mixture is too dry. Place in a crock, cover, and refrigerate. Garnish with parsley, and serve with good, crisp crackers, or on slices of rye bread.

DEVILED BEEF SPREAD

1 cup cooked beef, diced
1/4 cup mayonnaise
1 teaspoon dijon mustard
1 teaspoon worcestershire sauce
5 drops tabasco sauce
2 Tablespoons parsley, chopped
pepper to taste

Combine all of the ingredients in the work bowl of a food processor fitted with a steel blade and process until smooth and thoroughly blended. Place in a crock and cover with plastic. Chill before serving. A few lemon rinds on the top of the spread make a pretty presentation before everyone starts to dig in. Spread onto celery sticks or serve on crackers or the traditional toast triangles.

BEEF MOUSSE

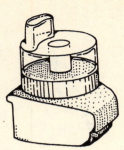

4 cups cooked roast beef, cubed and trimmed
1 chicken liver
1 clove garlic
2 Tablespoons parsley, chopped
2 cups light cream
4 Tablespoons butter

Preheat oven to 350°. Put all of the ingredients in the workbowl of
a food processor or blender and process until smooth and thoroughly
blended. Pour into a buttered shallow mold set into a pan of water.
Bake at 350° for 1 hour or until set. Allow mold to sit in water bath
for 10 minutes and unmold on a heated serving plate. With paper
towels, blot excess moisture from platter. Garnish with parsley and
serve with sour cream with some dried dill mixed into it.

HAM MOUSSE

3-3/4 cups bechamel sauce (see page 120)
1 cup cooked lean ham, ground
4 egg yolks
3/4 cup gruyere cheese, grated
1/2 cup heavy cream
1/4 teaspoon nutmeg
4 egg whites, beaten stiff

Preheat oven to 350°. Into 3 cups of bechamel sauce, stir the ham, egg
yolks, 1/4 cup of the gruyere cheese, and the cream. Season with
nutmeg, salt, and pepper to taste. Fold in stiffly beaten egg whites and
mix well. Pour into a buttered mold and bake at 350° in a pan of hot
water for 1 hour. After 1 hour or when well set, remove mold from
hot water and allow to sit in oven for 5 more minutes. Unmold onto
a heated, ovenproof platter, blotting any excess liquid with a paper
towel. Add the rest of the cheese to the reserved 3/4 cup of sauce and
pour over mousse. Return to oven and cook for 15 minutes more.

DEVILED HAM I

1 Tablespoon butter
3 Tablespoons onion, minced
1-1/2 Tablespoons flour
1-1/2 Tablespoons dry mustard
pinch of cayenne pepper
1/2 cup heavy cream, scalded
1 cup cooked ham, ground
1 Tablespoon dijon mustard
1-1/2 Tablespoons prepared horseradish, drained
pepper to taste
1 Tablespoon parsley, chopped
2 Tablespoons green pepper, finely chopped
1 teaspoon worcestershire sauce

In a saucepan, melt the butter and sauté the onion over a moderately high heat until soft. Stir in flour, mustard, and cayenne, and continue stirring for 3 more minutes. Remove the pan from heat. Pour in scalded cream, whisking vigorously until the mixture is thick and smooth. Return to heat and simmer for 15 minutes. In a bowl, combine the sauce, ham, dijon mustard, horseradish, and pepper. Add parsley, green pepper, and worcestershire sauce. Mix well. Chill for 2 hours or more. Restir the deviled ham and pack into a 1 cup crock. Serve with water crackers or French bread rounds.

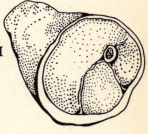

DEVILED HAM II

2 cups cooked ham, diced
2 Tablespoons mayonnaise
1-1/2 Tablespoons dijon mustard
1/4 teaspoon tabasco sauce

With the metal blade in place, add ham to work bowl of food processor. Turn machine on and off rapidly until a smooth paste is formed. Add mayonnaise, mustard and tabasco. Process until well blended. Place in a crock and cover. Refrigerate for 2 hours or more. Serve as an appetizer with celery and crackers.

PATÉS

The food processor is directly responsible for the wide range of pates I have been able to create from leftovers. The original experiment occurred one night after a dinner party when clearing the table I was confronted with a platter of sliced steak covered with mushrooms in garlic butter and garnished copiously with parsley. The food processor sitting conspicuously on the counter seemed an appealing alternative to sorting out bits of meat, congealed butter, and limp parsley. With a rubber spatula, I scraped the contents of the platter into the work bowl of the food processor and with the steel blade in place, mercilessly ground the mixture. I seasoned it with salt and pepper, packed it into a crock and refrigerated it overnight. The next day I served the paté with toasted slips of white bread, dijon mustard, and miniature pickles. It was delicious.

The varieties of patés are endless. I sometimes use herb flavored cream cheese (Boursin type). Alternate versions contain anchovy fillets, crème fraîche, mustard, mayonnaise, cognac, nuts, etc. I routinely feed the food processor after the family meal. Patés provide a use for soggy parsley which would otherwise be discarded and the parsley serves as an essential ingredient for most patés.

The methods for serving these spreads are also varied.

1. Paté and turkey sandwich on good black bread
2. Paté as a filling for cheese puffs
3. Paté served from the crock surrounded by crackers
4. Paté wrapped in puff pastry and baked

BASIC BEEF PATÉ

1 cup cooked beef (steak, roast, London broil)
8 Tablespoons butter
1/4 of a large onion
8 parsley sprigs
1/2 teaspoon salt
1/4 teaspoon pepper

Blend ingredients in a food processor or meat grinder until smooth. Taste for seasoning. Form into a loaf shape or place in a greased mold, cover with plastic wrap, and refrigerate. As an attractive garnish for serving, place thin strips of roasted red pepper across the top of the loaf. Surround the loaf with French bread and crackers.

COLD CUTS PATÉ

Leftover cold cuts such as salami, bologna,
or boiled ham
stone ground mustard
dill pickles, chopped

Put the cold cuts in the workbowl of the food processor fitted with a steel blade. Process the meats with an on off motion of the workbowl. Add enough stone ground mustard to make a homogenous mixture. Add chopped dill pickles to the workbowl and continue processing until the paté assumes the spiciness desired. Transfer the mixture to a crock. Cover with plastic wrap and refrigerate.

CHICKEN PATÉ

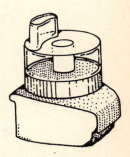

1-1/2 oz. boursin cheese
2 Tablespoons sweet butter
2 cups cooked chicken
1/8 teaspoon cayenne pepper
1/4 teaspoon coarse salt
3 scallion tops, chopped

In the workbowl of a food processor, with the steel blade in place, cream the cheese and butter. Add the chicken and mix until all is smooth and well combined. Add cayenne, salt, and scallion tops. Mix and taste, then adjust the seasonings. Remove to a small crock, and refrigerate until firm. Serve with sweet gerkins and a very solid cracker such as melba toast or stoned wheat crackers.

PATÉ MAISON

2 cups well done cooked beef
8 anchovy fillets
1 onion, cut in quarters
2 cloves garlic
1 teaspoon thyme, crushed
1 bay leaf, crumbled
salt & pepper to taste
8 Tablespoons butter
2 Tablespoons cognac
8 parsley sprigs

Using a food processor with the metal blade in place, add the beef,
anchovies, onion, garlic, thyme, bay leaf, salt, and pepper to the work
bowl. Turn on and off for 8 to 10 seconds or until all ingredients are
evenly chopped. Add butter and process until smooth. Add the
cognac and parsley. If additional butter is needed, add 1 Tablespoon
at a time. Process until smooth and thoroughly blended. Transfer the
mixture to a crock. Cover with plastic wrap and refrigerate. Serve with
crackers or French bread and small sweet pickles.

ACHRA
(A Trinidadian Favorite!)

2 cups cooked fish or tuna salad
2 eggs
1/2 cup flour
3 green onions, chopped
3 Tablespoons onion, chopped
4 Tablespoons parsley, chopped
pepper to taste

In a small bowl, mash fish with a fork. In a larger bowl, combine eggs,
flour, chopped onions, parsley, and pepper to taste. Add fish. Add
enough water to create a stiff batter. Form patties, and fry in hot oil.
Drain on paper towels. Garnish with fresh chopped parsley and
lemon wedges. Serve with tartar sauce.

RICE REMICK

1 cup cooked rice
1 cup cooked shrimp, small or cut in half if large
1/2 cup cooked peas
1-3/4 cups mayonnaise
1/2 cup chili sauce
few drops tabasco sauce
1/2 Tablespoon paprika
1 teaspoon dry mustard
1 teaspoon tarragon vinegar
4 slices crisp, cooked bacon, crumbled

Preheat oven to 350°. Grease 4 or 6 individual sized au gratin dishes with butter or margarine. Combine rice, shrimp and peas. Toss gently with a fork. In a separate bowl, combine mayonnaise, chili sauce, tabasco, paprika, mustard and vinegar. Blend half of the sauce into the rice mixture. Pile rice into prepared au gratin dishes. Heat in oven for 15 minutes and then top with crumbled bacon. Spread sauce over each and brown under a preheated broiler.

TUNA CRISPS

4 slices of white bread
1/4 cup mayonnaise
1-1/2 teaspoons onion, finely diced
1-1/2 teaspoons blue cheese
1/2 cup leftover tuna salad

Trim crusts from bread and slice on the diagonal. Toast the 8 bread pieces. Spread with tuna. Mix mayonnaise with onion and cheese. Top the tuna with mayonnaise mixture, covering bread entirely. Place diagonals on a cookie sheet. Put them under a broiler on the next to highest rack and watch constantly until brown and puffy. Serve as an appetizer or as a side dish with soup.

PICKLED FISH

3 Tablespoons lemon juice
1/3 cup olive oil
1/3 cup vegetable oil
1/4 teaspoon salt
1/4 teaspoon pepper
2 fried fillets of fish, each cut into 5 pieces
4 thin slices of red onion, separated into rings
2 Tablespoons parsley, finely chopped

Mix lemon juice and oils with salt and pepper. In a separate bowl, combine fish pieces, onion slices, and parsley. Add lemon juice and oil mixture. Refrigerate for 24 hours. Garnish with black olive circles and serve with crackers or on toast.

BEEF ROLLS

2 cups cooked pot roast, cubed
4 parsley sprigs
enough gravy or broth to moisten meat
8 Tablespoons butter
1 Tablespoon Madeira
salt & pepper to taste
8 slices of white bread, crusts removed
2 egg whites, lightly beaten
2 Tablespoons parmesan cheese, grated

Preheat oven to 375°. Put cubed pot roast and parsley in the workbowl of a food processor, and with steel blade in place, process until thoroughly blended. Add gravy or meat broth, 2 Tablespoons of melted butter, and the Madeira. Continue to process until a smooth paste is formed. Season to taste. With a rolling pin, flatten the bread slices. Spread each slice with the meat paste and roll them up, jelly roll style. Roll each in eggs and then parmesan. Set aside on a dish or waxed paper. Melt remaining 6 Tablespoons of butter and quickly coat each roll in melted butter. At this point the beef rolls may be frozen or put directly on a cookie sheet and baked at 375° until golden brown, turning once during baking. The rolls may be cut in half or in thirds. If frozen, cut before baking, and place them frozen in the preheated 375° oven until golden brown. Serve with a vegetable such as spinach which goes well with parmesan.

MEAT TURNOVERS

2 cups cooked steak, trimmed and ground
6 Tablespoons butter
3/4 cup beef stock
2 onions, finely chopped
2 Tablespoons flour
1 clove garlic, minced
1 teaspoon salt
pepper to taste
1 Tablespoon dried dill
1 package frozen Pepperidge Farm patty shells, defrosted
1 egg yolk blended with 1 Tablespoon water

Melt 3 Tablespoons of butter in a heavy skillet and brown the meat. Remove meat from pan and grind again or process with a steel blade of a food processor. Deglaze meat pan by adding beef stock and bringing to a boil. Set heated stock aside. In the same pan, brown onions in 3 Tablespoons of butter. Add flour and cook for 1 or 2 minutes, stirring constantly. Add stock and cook, stirring until thickened. Combine onion mixture with meat, dill, salt, and pepper to taste. Allow to cool. On a floured surface, roll each patty shell to 1/8" thickness, keeping the round shape. Divide the meat mixture equally between the 6 rounds. Fold the dough over the filling. Press the edges together with a fork. Prick top of crusts to allow for escape of steam. Place on a baking sheet and brush the tops with egg yolk mixture. Put the baking sheet in the freezer for 30 minutes. Preheat oven to 450°. Put baking sheet in oven and immediately turn it down to 400°. Bake for 30 to 40 minutes or until turnovers are golden brown.

SALAMI GOUGERE

1/3 cup water
2 Tablespoons sweet butter
1/4 teaspoon salt
1/2 cup flour
1/8 cup Swiss cheese
1/8 cup hard salami
3 green scallion tops
3 eggs

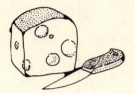

Preheat oven to 375°. Grease 12 miniature muffin cups with butter or margarine. In a saucepan, bring the water, butter, and salt to a boil. Remove from heat and stir in flour vigorously until it becomes a thick uniform paste. Set this sauce aside. In the workbowl of a food processor, with the steel blade intact, chop the cheese until it is fine. Set the chopped cheese aside, reserving 1 Tablespoon of the cheese for topping the finished puffs. Chop the salami and green scallion tops in the workbowl of the food processor until they are fine and combine with the grated cheese in a mixing bowl. Place the sauce in the workbowl with the steel knife still in place, and process continuously for 10 to 15 seconds. Remove lid of processor and crack in 2 of the eggs. Process continuously for 30 to 45 seconds. The mixture will be thick, smooth, and shiny. Add the salami, cheese, and scallions, and process with a few on off motions of the food processor until the mixture is well combined. DO NOT OVERPROCESS.

Spoon the mixture into the prepared muffin cups. Process the last egg in the food processor for 10 to 15 seconds. Paint the egg onto the puffs. Sprinkle the tops of the puffs with the remaining Tablespoon of cheese. Bake at 375° for 20 to 25 minutes or until puffed, brown, and dry. Allow to rest about 10 minutes out of the muffin tins before eating. Leftover puffs should be refrigerated and reheated in a 375° oven for 10 minutes. Note: Use 1-1/2 oz. of smoked salmon or ham in place of the salami. Also, gougere may be dropped on a greased cookie sheet for bite sized puffs, simply adjust baking time accordingly.

C H A P T E R

Vegetables & Side Dishes

THINGS TO COME IN...
Vegetables & Side Dishes

BROCCOLI/CAULIFLOWER AU GRATIN

1 Tablespoon butter
1 Tablespoon flour
2 cups half and half, scalded
salt & pepper to taste
pinch of nutmeg
2 cups cooked broccoli or cauliflower, chopped
1 cup gruyere cheese, coarsely grated
3 Tablespoons parmesan cheese, grated

Preheat oven to 325°. Melt butter in a heavy saucepan, add flour, and whisk for 2 minutes. Do not allow to color. Add scalded half and half in a stream, whisking vigorously. Simmer for 10 minutes. Add salt, pepper, and nutmeg and mix well. Mix in broccoli or cauliflower and cheese and turn all into a shallow baking dish. Sprinkle top with parmesan. Bake at 325° for 45 minutes or until browned and bubbly. Garnish with whole pine nuts or sliced almonds.

BLENDED SWEET PEAS

1 cup cooked peas, drained
1/4 cup heavy cream
1/4 cup sour cream
1/8 teaspoon sugar
pinch of nutmeg
1-1/2 teaspoons butter

Put peas and cream in a blender and mix thoroughly. Add the rest of the ingredients and continue to blend for several seconds. Place blended peas in top of double boiler with 1-1/2 teaspoons of butter and heat through. Garnish with mint.

MARINATED BRUSSEL SPROUTS

1 large clove garlic, finely chopped
1 Tablespoon dijon mustard
1/4 cup red wine vinegar
1/2 teaspoon coarse salt
1/2 teaspoon pepper
1 Tablespoon parsley, chopped
1/2 cup salad oil
1 cup cooked brussel sprouts

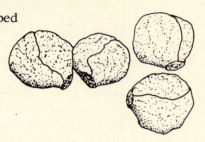

Combine garlic, mustard, vinegar, salt, pepper, and parsley. Whisk until thickened. Add oil in a slow steady stream, whisking constantly until mixture becomes thick and creamy. Pour dressing over cooked brussel sprouts, cover and refrigerate for several hours. Use the sprouts whole and by themselves or sliced into a salad. They can also be used as an appetizer with crackers or French bread rounds. Garnish with chopped walnuts or almonds for extra crunch.

BRUSSEL SPROUTS PURÉE OR SOUP

2 Tablespoons shallots, finely minced
2 Tablespoons sweet butter
1 cup cooked brussel sprouts, coarsely chopped
nutmeg to taste
salt & pepper to taste
1 egg, lightly beaten
1/4 cup heavy cream

In a skillet, sauté shallots in butter until softened. Add chopped brussel sprouts and seasonings. Cover and cook over a low heat for 8 minutes. Purée the brussel sprouts mixture in a food processor or a blender and add the egg and cream. Adjust the seasonings. To make this recipe a soup, add 2 cups of milk and heat until just about to boil. Garnish with croutons.

SWEET KRAUT SALAD

2 cups sauerkraut
1 cup celery, finely minced
1/2 cup green pepper, finely minced
1/2 medium onion, finely minced
1 small jar pimentos, drained and chopped
1-1/2 cups sugar

Toss everything except the sugar in a bowl until well blended. Place mixture in a large glass bowl and sprinkle sugar over mixture. DO NOT MIX. Cover and refrigerate overnight. Before serving, mix thoroughly until sugar is completely dissolved.

POTATO CHEESE BAKE

2 Tablespoons butter
1 clove garlic, chopped
1/4 cup onions, diced
1/4 cup mushrooms, sliced
1/4 cup sour cream
1/4 cup + 2 Tablespoons jack or cheddar cheese, grated
2 to 3 cups leftover mashed potatoes
1/4 teaspoon oregano
1/4 teaspoon basil
salt & pepper to taste

Preheat oven to 375°. Grease a 4 cup casserole dish with butter. In a skillet, melt butter and add garlic, onions, and mushrooms. Sauté until onion is soft. Combine cooked vegetables, sour cream, 1/4 cup cheese, and potatoes in a large mixing bowl. Add seasonings. Mix well, taste, and adjust seasonings. Pour into prepared casserole dish, smooth the top, and cover with remaining cheese. Bake at 375° for 20 minutes, until cheese turns light brown. Place under hot broiler for 2 minutes. Garnish with spring onion rounds.

HASH BROWN PIE
(Poor Man's Quiche)

1 prepared 9" pie crust
3 eggs, lightly beaten
1/2 cup light cream
1/2 teaspoon salt
1/4 teaspoon pepper
dash of nutmeg
1 cup leftover hash brown potatoes
10 oz. frozen spinach, chopped,
    cooked and drained
3 slices crisp, cooked bacon, crumbled
1/4 cup + 2 Tablespoons parmesan
    cheese, grated
2 cups cheese, grated (Use the heels of
    cheeses that are left in fridge. I like
    a combination of hearty swiss,
    sharp cheddar)
1 Tablespoon butter

Preheat oven to 350°. Roll pie crust to fit a 9" pan and set aside. Mix eggs, cream, salt, pepper, and nutmeg. Purée hash browns in food processor or blender. Add potatoes, spinach, bacon, 1/4 cup grated parmesan cheese, and other grated cheeses to the egg and cream mixture, whisking thoroughly but gently after each addition. Pour mixture into pie crust. Top with remaining 2 Tablespoons of parmesan cheese and dot with butter. Bake pie at 350° for 45 minutes to 1 hour or until nicely browned and puffy. Cut into wedges and serve. Notes: 1/4 cup of diced ham may be added in place of bacon, and leftover sliced mushrooms may be added. Different cheeses will change the flavor of the pie.

POTATOES FLORENTINE

5 eggs, separated
30 oz. frozen spinach, chopped,
    cooked and drained
6 Tablespoons melted butter
1/4 teaspoon nutmeg
salt & pepper to taste
1-1/2 cups leftover mashed potatoes,
    at room temperature
1 egg yolk
1/4 cup parmesan cheese, grated

Preheat oven to 375°. Grease a jelly roll pan with butter or margarine and cover the bottom with greased wax paper. Beat 5 yolks until lemon yellow and fluffy. Add spinach, butter, nutmeg, salt, and pepper to yolks and gently stir. Beat egg whites until stiff and fold into spinach mixture. Spread mixture onto wax paper, covering the bottom of the pan evenly. Bake at 375° for 15 to 18 minutes or until top springs back when touched. Turn jelly roll pan over on a damp tea towel and quickly peel off paper. (If not using immediately, roll the mixture, starting with the long side, in a tea towel and refrigerate.) Beat leftover mashed potatoes with 1 egg yolk and add salt and pepper to taste. (If using refrigerated spinach mixture, remove it from the refrigerator, and unroll it.) Spread the spinach mixture with the potatoes. Roll the combination together, starting with the long side, and chill it, wrapped in foil, for at least 1 hour. Preheat oven to 375°. Slice the roll in 1" slices and arrange the slices in a well buttered au gratin dish. Sprinkle the slices well with melted butter and parmesan cheese. Cover with foil. Bake slices at 375° for 25 minutes or until they are hot. Remove the foil and put the dish under the broiler for 2 to 3 minutes, or until the tops are brown.

MIXED VEGETABLE CURRY

2 cloves garlic, chopped
2 teaspoons ginger
1 teaspoon cinnamon
1 teaspoon coriander
1 teaspoon cumin
2 teaspoons tumeric
3 cardamon pods
1 teaspoon chili powder
1 teaspoon salt
1 Tablespoon oil
4 onions, sliced
2 cups hot water
1/2 cup parsley, minced
1 eggplant, cubed
4 carrots, cubed
4 potatoes, cubed
1/2 lb. unsweetened coconut (optional)
2 cups tomatoes
1/2 lb. peas or green beans

Mix the garlic and the spices in a bowl with a little water to make a paste. In a heavy pot or wok, heat oil very hot and add spices, cooking until slightly brown. Add onions and fry until tender. Add hot water, parsley, eggplant, carrots, and potatoes, and bring to a boil. Mix in coconut, tomatoes, peas or beans. Cover and simmer for about 30 minutes until vegetables are tender. Uncover and cook over high heat for 5 to 10 minutes until most of the liquid evaporates. You should end up with a thick gravy.

CAULIFLOWER CURRY

3 Tablespoons oil
2 cloves garlic, chopped
1/2 Tablespoon cloves, ground
1-1/2 teaspoons ginger
1/2 teaspoon tumeric
1/2 teaspoon cayenne pepper
1-1/2 Tablespoons cumin
1 teaspoon salt
1-1/2 cups onion, chopped
1 medium cauliflower, chopped
1/2 cup unsweetened coconut (optional)
1/4 cup water
3 Tablespoons lemon juice

In a heavy pot or wok, heat oil until it is very hot. Add garlic and spices. Sauté for a few seconds and add onions, cooking until tender. Add cauliflower, coconut, and water, and stir. Reduce heat and cover pan. Cook for 20 minutes, stirring occasionally, until cauliflower is tender. Increase to medium high heat and stir fry until slightly brown. Add 1 Tablespoon oil during this process if too dry. Add lemon juice, toss and serve. Serve as main curry or second curry with other meat and vegetable curries.

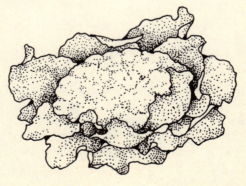

CURRIED RICE

4 Tablespoons butter
2 teaspoons curry powder
2 Tablespoons onion, minced
1 Tablespoon pine nuts
1/2 cup golden raisins, plumped
2 cups cooked rice

Grease a 2 cup mold. Melt butter in skillet, and cook curry powder over a low heat for 2 to 3 minutes, stirring constantly. Add onions and cook until translucent. Add pine nuts and cook until golden. Stir in raisins and warm briefly. Remove pan from heat and, with a fork, stir in rice completely. Mix until each grain is coated with the curry mixture. Pack the rice tightly into the prepared mold. Cover the top of the mold with a buttered piece of waxed paper, and place it on a rack in a pot filled with 2" of water. Cover the pot and steam over a low heat until hot. Unmold on a heated serving platter.

PORK FRIED RICE

1/4 teaspoon sugar
2-1/2 teaspoons soy sauce
1 teaspoon oyster sauce
3 Tablespoons peanut oil
1 cup cooked rice
1 egg, lightly beaten
1/4 teaspoon salt
1/4 cup scallions, sliced thinly (reserve
      some for garnish)
1/2 cup cooked roast pork, diced

Mix sugar with soy and oyster sauces in a small cup. Place wok or frying pan over high flame for 30 seconds. Add peanut oil to the heated wok or pan, and heat until oil is hot but not smoking. Add rice and stir fry for 2 minutes. Add sauce mixture and stir for 1 minute. Add egg and mix it all around with the rice. Sprinkle with salt, and add scallions and pork. Stir fry for 1 more minute or until hot. Serve at once. Garnish with scallion slices.

SOUFFLÉS

Although soufflés are reputably temperamental, they are actually quite easy to make. The secret to a good soufflé is in the beating and folding of the egg whites. As long as you follow a few simple rules, your soufflé will always receive rave reviews. It is critical that the egg whites be at room temperature when they are beaten, and they should be beaten until stiff, but not dry. It is also important that they be folded into the soufflé base, not stirred in. The best way to fold them is to first pour half of the beaten egg whites onto the top of the mixture. Then, with a spoon, slowly move through the mixture in a motion away from you, to the bottom of the bowl, and back up through the mixture in a motion towards you. After completing this motion a few times, add the rest of the beaten egg whites, and repeat until thoroughly blended. The other trick is to serve soufflés at once, and that way, they won't have a chance to fall. In my opinion, soufflés are best served with a good green salad with a vinaigrette or mustard dressing, and very fresh Italian or French bread.

BROCCOLI SOUFFLÉ

3 Tablespoons butter
3 Tablespoons flour
1 cup milk, scalded
3 eggs, separated
1/2 cup parmesan cheese, freshly grated
6 oz. cooked broccoli, chopped
a few grinds of nutmeg
salt & pepper to taste

Preheat oven to 425°. Grease a 4 cup soufflé dish with butter or margarine. Coat the bottom and sides of the dish with part of the parmesan cheese and refrigerate. In a saucepan, melt the butter. Add the flour and stir until a smooth roux is formed. Cook the roux over a very low heat for 2 to 3 minutes. Do not allow it to brown. Add the scalded milk to the roux in a steady stream, whisking continuously until the mixture is smooth and thickened. Cook the sauce for a few minutes over a low heat, stirring with a wooden spoon.

Beat the yolks until light and lemon colored. Add the yolks to the sauce and stir until the mixture is well combined. Add cheese, broccoli, nutmeg, salt, and pepper to the sauce, stirring well. Beat the egg whites until stiff but not dry. Whisk about 1/4 of the egg whites into the broccoli mixture. Fold the rest of the egg whites in very gently, but thoroughly. Pour the mixture into the prepared soufflé dish. Wipe the edges of the dish clean. Bake at 425° for 15 to 20 minutes.

CAULIFLOWER SOUFFLÉ

1/4 cup spring onions, sliced (reserve some for
    garnish)
4 Tablespoons butter
3 Tablespoons flour
1 cup milk, scalded
4 egg yolks
1 cup sharp cheddar cheese, shredded
3/4 cup parmesan cheese, grated
1 cup cooked cauliflower, chopped
1 teaspoon salt
1/2 teaspoon worcestershire sauce
3 dashes tabasco sauce
6 egg whites

Preheat oven to 400°. Prepare a 1-1/2 quart soufflé dish by buttering the dish and sprinkling it with parmesan cheese on the sides and bottom. In a skillet, sauté spring onions in 1 Tablespoon of butter until soft. In another sauce pan, melt 3 Tablespoons of butter, adding the flour to make a roux, and cook, stirring constantly, for 3 minutes. Add the scalded milk all at one time to the roux, whisking vigorously. Cook until thickened. Beat the egg yolks one at a time into the sauce. Add the cheddar cheese and 1/4 cup of the parmesan, and cook until just melted. Stir in the cooked onions and cauliflower and blend well. Add the salt, worcestershire, and tabasco sauces.

In a mixing bowl, beat the egg whites until they hold soft peaks. Stir about 1/3 of them into the cauliflower mixture, blend thoroughly, and gently fold in the rest of the egg whites. Pour mixture into the prepared soufflé dish, smooth the top, and sprinkle with the remaining parmesan cheese. Place in the oven and immediately reduce heat to 375°. Bake for 20 to 30 minutes. Garnish with sliced spring onions. Serve at once.

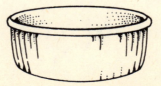

POTATO SOUFFLÉ

1-1/2 cups leftover mashed potatoes
1/3 cup heavy cream
3 egg yolks, lightly beaten
4 egg whites
1/4 teaspoon cream of tartar
3 Tablespoons gruyere cheese, grated
pinch of nutmeg
salt & white pepper to taste

Preheat oven to 375°. Grease a 1-1/2 quart casserole or soufflé dish with butter or margarine. Beat potatoes with cream and season with nutmeg, salt and pepper. Cook mixture in saucepan over low heat to avoid scorching, until potatoes are very hot. Remove from heat and add cheese. Add 3 beaten egg yolks one at a time, beating well after each addition. If there are lumps, pass through a sieve. Add cream of tartar and a pinch of salt to the 4 egg whites, and beat until they are stiff but not dry. Fold gently but thoroughly into the potato mixture. Place mixture into the prepared baking dish. Bake at 375° for 30 minutes. Garnish with dried dill. Serve at once. This is a wonderful side dish for any type of meat, although I would serve it with a sauceless dish so as not to completely overload on calories.

CHICKEN SOUFFLÉ

7 Tablespoons butter
2 Tablespoons onion, minced
6 Tablespoons flour
2 cups chicken stock, scalded
1/2 cup parmesan cheese, grated
1/2 teaspoon salt
1/2 teaspoon pepper
1/2 teaspoon tarragon
1 Tablespoon parsley, chopped
4 egg yolks, lightly beaten
1 cup mushrooms, thinly sliced
1-1/2 cups cooked chicken, finely chopped
pinch of salt
1/8 teaspoon cream of tartar
5 egg whites
1/2 cup heavy cream

Preheat oven to 375°. Grease a 2 quart soufflé dish with butter or margarine and coat with parmesan cheese. Melt butter in a heavy sauce pan, add minced onion, and sauté until soft. Add flour and whisk vigorously for 3 minutes. Add scalded stock in a stream, stirring constantly until thick and smooth. Simmer for 15 minutes. Remove from heat. Remove 1 cup of sauce and add to that 2 Tablespoons of parmesan. Cover the sauce and cheese mixture with a buttered round of waxed paper and set aside. To the remaining sauce, add salt, pepper, tarragon, and parsley. Then add egg yolks one at a time, beating well after each addition. Sauté the mushrooms in the remaining butter, and add them to the chicken in as large bowl. Pour the sauce over the chicken mixture. Add a pinch of salt and cream of tartar to the egg whites, and beat until stiff. Fold the egg whites gently into the chicken mixture. DO NOT OVERMIX. Pour the entire mixture into the prepared soufflé dish, smooth the top, and bake at 375° for 30 to 40 minutes or until nicely puffed and brown. Just before serving, heat reserved sauce. Season sauce with salt and pepper to taste, and stir in heavy cream. Bring just to the boiling point. Serve with saffron rice.

CHEESE SOUFFLÉ ROLL FILLED WITH BEEF

For Cheese Soufflé:
5-1/3 Tablespoons butter
1 Tablespoon onion, minced
6 Tablespoons flour
1-1/4 cups milk, scalded
1/2 teaspoon + a pinch salt
7 eggs, separated
pinch of cayenne pepper
1/2 teaspoon worcestershire sauce
1/2 cup sharp cheddar cheese, coarsely grated
1/2 cup parmesan cheese, coarsely grated
1/4 teaspoon cream of tartar

For Beef Filling:
1/4 cup onion, finely chopped
3 Tablespoons butter
2 cups cooked roast beef, ground
salt & pepper to taste
1/4 cup sharp cheddar cheese, grated
1/4 cup parsley, chopped (optional)
3/4 cup sour cream

For Cheese Sauce:
1-1/2 Tablespoons butter
1-1/2 Tablespoons flour
1-1/2 cups light cream, scalded
1/4 cup sharp cheddar cheese, grated
dash of worcestershire sauce
salt & pepper to taste

To Make Soufflé:
Preheat oven to 300°. Grease a jelly roll pan with butter or margarine. Line the bottom with waxed paper and grease with butter. Melt butter in a heavy sauce pan. Add onion and sauté until soft. With a wire whisk, stir in flour and sauté, without coloring for 2 to 3 minutes. Add scalded milk in a stream, whisking vigorously until thick and smooth and mixture leaves the bottom of the pan. Stir in 1/2 teaspoon salt, cayenne, and worcestershire sauce. Beat in cheeses. Add egg yolks one at a time, beating well after each addition. Cool the mixture. Beat egg whites with a pinch of salt and the cream of tartar until they form

stiff peaks when beater is raised. Fold egg whites into the cheese mixture, gently but thoroughly. Spread evenly into the prepared jelly roll pan. Bake at 300° for 15 minutes. Remove from oven at the end of the 15 minutes.

To Make Beef Filling:
In a heavy saucepan, sauté onion in butter until transparent and lightly colored. Add ground beef, stirring constantly to prevent sticking. Add grated cheese and combine completely with meat mixture. Add salt, pepper and parsley and blend mixture with the sour cream. Set aside to cool.

To Assemble:
Preheat oven to 375°. Loosen edges of cooled soufflé, and invert on waxed paper sprinkled lightly with parmesan cheese. Peel off top layer of waxed paper. Spread surface of soufflé evenly with beef filling. Roll up the soufflé with the beef filling, jelly roll style from the long side. Place filled soufflé roll on a greased cookie sheet, sprinkle with grated cheddar cheese and cover loosely with foil. Bake at 375° for 15 minutes or until hot. Remove foil and brown soufflé under the broiler for 1 or 2 minutes. With a large spatula, remove to serving dish or board. If desired, serve with cheese sauce.

To Make Cheese Sauce:
Melt butter over low heat, blending in flour and whisking for about 2 minutes. Remove from heat. Add scalded cream to the flour mixture all at once, whisking vigorously. Set pan over high heat and keep whisking until it comes to a boil. Lower heat and simmer for about 5 minutes. Add cheddar cheese, worcestershire sauce, salt and pepper to taste, and stir until cheese melts.

BEEF SOUFFLÉ

3 Tablespoons butter
3 Tablespoons flour
1-1/2 cups milk, scalded
1/3 cup parmesan cheese, grated
2/3 cup cheddar cheese, grated
3 drops tabasco sauce
1 teaspoon worcestershire sauce
salt & pepper to taste
6 egg yolks, lightly beaten
1-1/2 cups cooked beef, finely chopped
2 shallots, finely chopped
pinch of salt
1/8 teaspoon cream of tartar
8 egg whites

Preheat oven to 375°. Grease an 8 cup soufflé dish with butter or margarine. Melt butter in a heavy saucepan. Add the flour, and whisk the roux over a very low heat for 3 or 4 minutes. Do not allow it to color. Stir in the scalded milk in a stream and whisk until mixture is thick and bubbly. Stir in cheeses and seasonings. Cook only until cheese is melted. Remove from heat and stir in egg yolks one at a time, whisking thoroughly. Stir meat and shallots into mixture. Set aside to cool. Add a pinch of salt and the cream of tartar to the egg whites, and beat until stiff. Fold egg whites into the beef mixture. Gently pour mixture into the prepared soufflé dish, and smooth the top. Bake at 375° for 25 to 30 minutes or until puffed and golden.

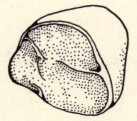

SOUFFLÉ LORRAINE

3-1/2 Tablespoons butter
4 Tablespoons flour
1-1/2 cups milk, scalded
pinch of cayenne pepper
1/8 teaspoon dry mustard
dash worcestershire sauce
1 cup cooked ham, minced
1/2 cup Swiss cheese, grated
1/2 cup gruyere or parmesan
    cheese, grated
5 egg yolks, lightly beaten
6 egg whites
1/8 teaspoon cream of tartar

Preheat oven to 375°. Grease a 6 cup soufflé dish with butter or margarine and coat the bottom and sides with parmesan cheese. Melt butter in a heavy saucepan, add flour and stir with a wire whisk until well blended. Continue cooking and stirring for 3 minutes over very low heat. Remove pan from heat and add the scalded milk all at once, stirring vigorously. Return to heat and simmer for 10 minutes. Add cayenne, dry mustard, and worcestershire sauce, and blend. Add the ham and cheese, mix again. Remove the pan from heat. Add the yolks one at a time to the mixture, and mix thoroughly after each addition. Add the cream of tartar to the egg whites, and beat until stiff. Fold into the mixture. Pour the mixture into the prepared soufflé dish. Smooth the top of the soufflé and sprinkle it with parmesan cheese. Bake at 375° for 30 to 45 minutes.

CHAPTER 6

Salads & Light Fare

THINGS TO COME IN...
Salads & Light Fare

SALADS

Salad can take on many faces, as a delectible palate cleanser, a side dish, or a veritable meal. Every salad, however, should have a fresh taste with a bit of a tang. Any lettuce used should be dry (dressing won't stick to wet leaves), raw vegetables should be crisp, cooked vegetables should not be soggy, and meat should have all visible fat removed. Unless it is rice based, salad should always be dressed and tossed right before serving to keep it fresh tasting. As far as presentation is concerned, serve most salads chilled, but not cold, on chilled plates or bowls.

CLASSIC RICE SALAD

3 cups cooked rice
1/2 green pepper, diced
1/2 red pepper, diced
6 scallions, sliced in rounds

For the Vinaigrette:
1 teaspoon kosher salt
1/2 teaspoon pepper
1/4 cup wine vinegar
1/2 cup + 1 Tablespoon olive oil

Mix rice with vegetables. In a separate bowl, combine the dressing ingredients. Toss the rice mixture with the vinaigrette. Pack tightly in a ceramic mold and chill for 1 hour or more. Unmold on a serving platter. Garnish with freshly chopped basil or more of the sliced scallions, using the green tops only.

IMPERIAL RICE SALAD

2 cups cooked rice
1/2 cup cooked sweet peas or any leftover green vegetable
1/2 cup cooked pork, diced

For the Sauce:
1 cup mayonnaise
3 Tablespoons chili sauce
1 clove garlic, minced
1 teaspoon dry tarragon
1/2 teaspoon dry mustard
1 hardboiled egg, finely chopped
1 Tablespoon parsley or coriander, chopped
1 Tablespoon capers, rinsed and patted dry

Combine rice, peas, and pork, very gently tossing with a fork. Refrigerate. Mix the remaining ingredients together to make the sauce. Toss the two mixtures together and refrigerate for a few hours. Serve cold or at room temperature on a bed of lettuce leaves with sliced or chopped tomatoes on the side.

SALAD NICOISE

15 oz. tuna, drained or leftover cooked chicken or shrimp
2 large potatoes, boiled or baked, and sliced
6 olives, halved, pitted, and cut into strips
1/2 cup cooked green or lima beans
2 hard boiled eggs, chopped
2 anchovies, minced (optional)

For the Dressing:
3 Tablespoons wine vinegar
1 clove garlic, put through a press
1 teaspoon dijon mustard
1/2 teaspoon kosher salt
1/2 teaspoon pepper
1/2 cup olive oil

Place crumbled tuna, or chopped chicken or shrimp in a bowl. Add sliced potatoes, olives, beans, eggs, and anchovies. To make the dressing, put vinegar in a bowl and whisk in the garlic, mustard, salt, and pepper. Pour in olive oil and whisk until thick. Pour over salad mixture and correct the seasonings. Allow to marinate for 1 hour or more before serving. Arrange on a platter by mounding the salad mixture in the center and surrounding it with sliced beets and beans.

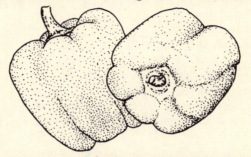

TUNA, RED PEPPER & RICE SALAD

3 cups cooked rice
14 oz. canned tuna, packed in oil
1 red pepper, diced
1/2 cup onion, chopped
6 black olives, pitted and quartered
1 Tablespoon capers (optional)
2 Tablespoons parsley, chopped
2 cloves garlic, put through a press
2 Tablespoons parmesan cheese, grated

For the Dressing:
1 teaspoon dijon mustard
1/2 cup red wine vinegar
1/2 cup salad oil
salt & pepper to taste

Combine rice, tuna, red pepper, onions, olives, capers, parsley, garlic, and parmesan cheese. Toss lightly with a fork. In a separate bowl, mix mustard, vinegar, and oil thoroughly. Pour dressing over the rice mixture and mix gently with a fork. Add salt and pepper to taste. Allow to stand for 1 hour. Mix again before serving. Serve on a bed of lettuce or a purple cabbage leaf, and garnish with black olives, pitted and cut in half.

FISH SALAD

1-1/2 Tablespoons onion, finely chopped
2 teaspoons parsley, chopped
1 Tablespoon dill pickle, finely chopped
1 teaspoon lemon juice
1 cup mayonnaise
1 cup cooked fish
1/4 cup celery, chopped
1 hardboiled egg, chopped

Combine onion, parsley, pickle, and lemon juice with mayonnaise. Combine the remaining ingredients and use as much of the mayonnaise mixture as necessary to bind the salad. Serve the extra mayonnaise mixture on the side. Grated lemon peel is a fitting garnish.

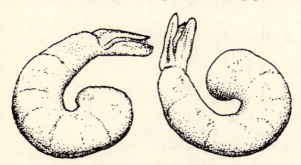

SHRIMP SALAD

1/2 cup mayonnaise
2 Tablespoons onion, minced
1/8 cup chili sauce
1 cup cooked shrimp, chopped into large pieces
1/2 avocado, diced
1/4 cup celery, sliced thin
2 springs fresh dill or 1/4 teaspoon dried dill
salt & pepper to taste

Mix mayonnaise, onion, and chili sauce in a large bowl. Add shrimp, avocado, and celery, and toss together lightly. Snip dill into the bowl and season with salt and pepper. Serve on shredded lettuce with pita bread.

CHEF SALAD

Assorted Salad Materials:
lettuce
tomatoes
cucumbers
bell pepper
hardboiled eggs
leftover ham
Swiss cheese
3 spring onions, sliced into rounds
8 parsley sprigs, chopped
1/4 of a medium onion, minced

For the Dressing:
1-1/2 cups mayonnaise
1/4 cup chili sauce
2 Tablespoons prepared
     horseradish, drained
1 Tablespoon capers, drained (optional)
1 teaspoon lemon juice
1 teaspoon sugar
1 teaspoon worcestershire sauce
salt & pepper to taste

Blend all dressing ingredients well and set aside. Cut ham and Swiss into matchstick like pieces. Toss all salad ingredients together, dress with salad dressing and toss again. Using 6 or 8 pieces of cheese and ham, cross them across the top of the salad. Serve as a main course with a good bread.

TURKEY WALDORF SALAD

2 cups cooked turkey, shredded
1 large tart apple (I like Granny Smith and pippin), diced
2 celery ribs, sliced
1 cup walnuts, chopped
1/2 cup golden raisins

For the Dressing:
1-1/2 cups plain yogurt
1 Tablespoon orange zest, grated
2 teaspoons tarragon
salt & pepper to taste

In salad bowl, combine turkey, apple, celery, walnuts, and raisins. In a separate bowl, mix together the dressing ingredients. Pour the dressing over the salad, and toss well to coat. Adjust seasonings to taste. Garnish with mandarin orange slices. Serve with leftover cranberries.

TURKEY & WILD RICE SALAD

3 cups cooked turkey, cubed
2 cups cooked wild rice
1 small onion, finely chopped
1/2 cup slivered almonds, toasted
2 tomatoes, cut in wedges
2 hardboiled eggs, cut in wedges

For the Dressing:
1 cup mayonnaise
1/4 cup wine vinegar
1/2 teaspoon dry mustard
2 Tablespoons dijon mustard

Toss turkey and wild rice. Chill for 30 minutes. Remove from refrigerator and add chopped onion and almonds. Mix together the dressing ingredients. Toss rice mixture with dressing and taste for seasoning. Serve on lettuce leaves and garnish by circling with the egg and tomato wedges. Cold leftover peas are a good addition to this salad.

CHICKEN SALAD VERONIQUE

2 cups cooked chicken, cubed
1/2 cup celery, diced
1/3 cup seedless grapes, halved
2 scallions, sliced in rounds
1/4 cup slivered almonds
salt & pepper to taste
2 dashes worcestershire sauce
1/2 cup mayonnaise
1/2 teaspoon curry powder

Combine the chicken, celery, grapes, scallions, and almonds in a bowl. Season with salt and pepper. Sprinkle with worcestershire sauce. In a separate bowl, combine mayonnaise and curry powder. Bind the chicken mixture with the curry mayonnaise, tossing lightly. Serve on a lettuce leaf. Garnish with mandarin oranges, either by circling a scoop of the salad with them or by setting a portion of them off to the side of the lettuce leaf.

CURRIED CHICKEN SALAD

3/4 cup mayonnaise
1/2 teaspoon curry powder
1-1/2 Tablespoons chutney
1 Tablespoon onion, finely minced
1-1/2 cups chicken, cubed
1 cup canned chick peas, rinsed and drained
1/2 cup slivered almonds

Combine mayonnaise with curry powder, onion, and chutney. Mix well. Combine chicken, chick peas, and almonds. Coat chicken mixture well with the mayonnaise mixture. Chill and serve. If you can, get some fresh coriander and chop it to mix into the salad or use as a garnish. Pita or pumpernickel would be good choices for bread.

CHICKEN & ZUCCHINI SALAD WITH
MUSTARD DRESSING

2 cups cooked chicken, cut in matchstick pieces
2 cups zucchini, cut in matchstick pieces
1/2 cup Swiss cheese, coarsely grated

For the Dressing:
2 Tablespoons onion, finely chopped
1 Tablespoon kosher salt
1 large clove garlic, minced
3 Tablespoons lemon juice
1 Tablespoon French country style mustard
1/3 cup vegetable oil
1/3 cup olive oil
pepper to taste

Combine chicken, zucchini, and cheese. In a blender or the work bowl of a food processor fitted with the steel knife, combine onion, salt, garlic, lemon juice, and mustard. Process until thick and thoroughly mixed. Add the oils in a slow, steady stream, and process until well blended. Pour the dressing over the chicken mixture and toss. Taste, adjust seasonings, and allow to stand for 1 or 2 hours before serving. Garnish with grated carrot.

CURRIED PORK SALAD

3/4 cup mayonnaise
1/2 cup curry powder
1 Tablespoon chutney
2 cups lean cooked pork, cubed
1/4 cup tart apple, chopped
1/4 cup slivered almonds, toasted
2 Tablespoons parsley, chopped
salt & pepper to taste

Combine mayonnaise with curry powder and chutney. Toss pork, apple, almonds, and parsley. Bind with mayonnaise mixture. Season to taste with salt and pepper. Chill for about 1 hour and serve. Garnish with chopped apple, leaving the skin on for color.

LAMB SALAD

2 cups cooked lamb, cut into matchstick pieces
1/2 cup boiled potatoes, diced
1/2 cup cooked carrots, diced
1/4 cup cooked peas
2 Tablespoons onions, finely chopped
1/4 cup lemon juice
salt & pepper to taste
1/4 cup mayonnaise
2 teaspoons dijon mustard

Combine lamb, potatoes, carrots, peas, onions, and lemon juice. Add salt and pepper to taste. Allow mixture to sit, covered, at room temperature, for 1 hour. Mix the mayonnaise with the mustard, and fold into the lamb mixture. Adjust seasonings and add more lemon juice to taste. Serve on lettuce or cabbage leaves garnished with hard cooked eggs, tomato slices, and chopped mint, which is fabulous on any lamb dish

CHICKEN CROQUETTES

3 cups bechamel sauce (see page 119)
1-1/2 cups cooked chicken, coarsely diced
1-1/2 Tablespoons fresh parsley, chopped
1 egg, lightly beaten
seasoned bread crumbs
1 cup vegetable oil

Combine 1-1/2 cups of the bechamel sauce with the chicken and parsley, and chill. When cold, roll into sausage shapes and cut into 2" lengths. Dip in beaten egg and then roll in the bread crumbs. Chill for 1 hour. Heat oil in a pan, about 2" deep, to 380°. Fry the croquettes, turning until evenly browned. Drain on paper towels. Serve with the reserved, warmed bechamel sauce.

LAMB CROQUETTES

2 cups cooked lamb, finely chopped
2 cups soubise sauce (see page 122)
2 egg yolks
1/2 teaspoon parsley, finely chopped
1 teaspoon worcestershire sauce
1/2 teaspoon dry mustard
salt & pepper to taste
1 cup flour
1 egg, lightly beaten with 1 Tablespoon water
1 cup dry seasoned bread crumbs
1 cup vegetable oil

Combine lamb with 1 cup of soubise sauce, 2 egg yolks, parsley, worcestershire sauce, dry mustard, salt, and pepper. Spread 1/2" thick on a buttered cookie sheet and chill, covered, for about 2 hours. Divide the mixture into 12 equal portions and form into cylinders. Dust the croquettes with flour, coat with egg and water wash, and roll them in bread crumbs. Heat oil in a skillet to about 380° and fry until golden. Drain on paper towels Serve with reserved soubise sauce, warm pita wedges, and any simple green vegetable.

CRÊPES

Crêpes make a perfect vehicle for using leftovers. Make a batch of crêpes according to the basic recipe, freeze them and use them as needed with suggested fillings.

BASIC CRÊPES

3/4 cup flour, sifted
3/4 teaspoon salt
3/4 cup water
2/3 cup milk
3 eggs
2 Tablespoons butter,
    melted and cooled

In a blender, blend all of the ingredients for 5 seconds. Turn off the motor, and with a rubber spatula, scrape down the sides of the container. Blend for 20 seconds more. Transfer the batter to a bowl and let it stand, covered with plastic wrap, for 1 hour.

Heat a 7" iron crêpe pan on moderately high heat until it is hot. Brush the pan lightly with clarified butter or oil. Heat until hot, but not smoking. Remove the pan from the heat. Stir the batter. Half fill a 1/4 cup measuring cup with some batter. Pour the batter into the pan. Tilt and rotate the pan so that the batter covers the bottom in a thin layer. Return any excess batter to the bowl. Return the pan to the heat, loosen the edge of the crêpe from the pan and cook until the underside of the crêpe is lightly browned. Turn the crêpe and brown the other side. Make crêpes in the same manner with the remaining batter, brushing the pan with clarified butter or oil as needed. Put sheets of plastic wrap between crêpes and wrap the stacked crêpes in plastic wrap. Freeze or refrigerate and use as needed. Frozen crêpes will thaw unwrapped at room temperature in 10 to 15 minutes. Crêpes can be reheated in a 300° oven a few minutes before filling.

Some suggestions for breakfast crêpe fillings:
1. Sliced fresh fruit, coated in brown sugar with whipped cream on top
2. Diced cooked vegetables with grated cheese melted over the top
3. Grated cheeses mixed with herbs and spices

CHICKEN FILLING FOR CRÊPES

3 Tablespoons sweet butter
1 Tablespoon shallots, finely minced
2 Tablespoons flour
1 cup strong chicken stock, scalded
salt & pepper to taste
1 Tablespoon Madeira
1 cup cooked chicken, finely minced
4 Tablespoons gruyere cheese, freshly grated
1 cup crème fraîche

Grease a shallow baking dish with butter or maragrine. In a heavy saucepan, melt the butter. Add the shallots and cook until limp and transparent. Add in the flour, stirring constantly. Cook over a low heat for 2 to 3 minutes. Do not allow the mixture to brown. Add scalded chicken stock to the flour mixture in a steady stream. Cook until thickened and bubbly. Season with salt and pepper. Add the Madeira, taste, and adjust the seasonings. Add the chicken and 2 Tablespoons cheese. Mix thoroughly and remove from the heat to cool. Preheat oven to 350°. When the chicken mixture is cool, place 2 Tablespoons of it on each crêpe. Roll up crêpes and place in prepared baking dish. Mask the crêpes with the crème fraîche and sprinkle with the remaining 2 Tablespoons of cheese. Bake at 350° for 10 to 15 minutes and then run under a hot broiler for 2 to 3 minutes to brown the cheese.

HAM FILLING FOR CRÊPES

3 Tablespoons butter
1/2 cup mushrooms, finely minced
1 Tablespoon onion, finely chopped
2 Tablespoons flour
1 cup whole milk, scalded
1 cup cooked ham, finely minced
1 teaspoon dijon mustard
2 Tablespoons parmesan cheese, freshly grated
1/8 teaspoon nutmeg
2 Tablespoons parsley, finely chopped
salt & pepper to taste

Grease a shallow baking dish with butter or margarine. In a heavy saucepan, over a moderate heat, melt the butter. Add the mushrooms and onions and cook until the onions are wilted and transparent. Stir in the flour, stirring constantly. Cook the roux over a low heat for 2 to 3 minutes. Do not allow roux to brown. Add the scalded milk all at once in a stream, whisking vigorously until the mixture begins to bubble and thicken. Add the ham, mustard, 1 Tablespoon of the parmesan cheese, nutmeg, parsley, and salt and pepper to taste. Allow mixture to cool. Preheat oven to 400°. Lay each crêpe separately on a work surface. Place 2 Tablespoons of the cooled ham mixture on each one. Fold the crêpe over the filling and roll it up. Place the crêpes in prepared baking dish and sprinkle the crêpes with the remaining Tablespoon of parmesan cheese. Bake at 400° for 10 to 15 minutes until warm.

CURRIED PORK FILLING FOR CRÊPES

3 Tablespoons butter
1 Tablespoon curry powder
1 Tablespoon onion, finely chopped
2 Tablespoons flour
1 cup milk, scalded
salt & pepper to taste
1 cup cooked pork, finely minced
1/4 cup unsalted roasted peanuts, coarsely chopped
peach chutney

Grease a shallow baking dish with butter or margarine. Melt butter in a heavy saucepan, stir in curry powder, add onion, and sauté until limp and transparent. Add flour and cook for 2 to 3 minutes over a low heat. Add scalded milk in a slow, steady stream. Cook until thick and bubbly. Season to taste with salt and pepper. Add pork and allow to cool. Preheat oven to 400°. Stir in chopped peanuts to cooled mixture. Lay each crêpe separately on a work surface. Place 2 Tablespoons of the pork mixture on each one, and roll them up. Arrange crêpes in prepared baking dish and bake at 400° for 10 to 15 minutes. Spoon peach chutney over the crêpes and serve at once.

SLICED TURKEY WITH TONNATO SAUCE

7 oz. canned tuna, packed in oil
5 anchovies
1 Tablespoon lemon juice
1 cup mayonnaise
1 large clove garlic, minced
pepper to taste
leftover turkey slices

In a food processor or a blender, combine the tuna and its oil with the anchovies, lemon juice, mayonnaise, and garlic. Process until mixture is very smooth. Taste, and adjust seasonings. Heat until just warm and serve over heated turkey slices. Garnish with capers and lemon slices. Serve with a cold rice salad with a vinaigrette dressing.

MARINATED BEEF SLICES

leftover cooked steak, thinly sliced
1/2 cup red wine
1/2 cup soy sauce
1/8 cup olive oil
3 Tablespoons lemon juice
1 Tablespoon dijon mustard
1/4 cup worcestershire sauce
1 clove garlic, crushed
salt & pepper to taste

Marinate leftover steak in all of the other ingredients for 2 hours or even overnight. Drain marinade off and broil slices for 2 or 3 minutes until hot. Serve with pickles as an appetizer, or on garlic bread for a delicious sandwich. Slice into matchstick size pieces and use in a mixed green salad. For breakfast, serve with hash browns and fried eggs.

DEVILED BEEF OR BEEF BONES

bones left from a rib roast with some meat left on them (accumulate
    enough of these in the freezer until you have a substantial
    amount to serve) or substitute cooked beef, sliced
2 eggs, beaten until frothy
fine bread crumbs
6 Tablespoons beef drippings or butter
1-1/2 cups sauce diable (see page 121)

Dip the beef or bones in the egg, coating them well, and then into
the bread crumbs until they are well coated. Melt the butter or beef
drippings in a skillet and cook the beef or bones until the crumbs are
crusty and brown and the meat is hot. Serve with the sauce diable.
The bones may also be broiled under a low flame until crispy.

BARBECUED BEEF ON BUNS

1 12 oz. bottle of chili sauce and an equal amount of water
3 heaping Tablespoons brown sugar
2 Tablespoons vinegar
salt & pepper to taste
1 Tablespoon worcestershire sauce
1 clove garlic, put through a press
juice of one lemon
1 Tablespoon soy sauce
3 cups well cooked beef, diced or shredded

Combine all ingredients except the meat. Stir thoroughly, and
over moderate heat, cook for 30 minutes. Add the meat and cook for
another 30 minutes. Taste and adjust seasonings. Serve on hamburger
buns with cole slaw and shoestring potatoes, or over rice and covered
with grated sharp cheddar cheese.

BARBECUED PORK ON BUNS

1 14 oz. bottle of ketchup
1/2 cup water
1 Tablespoon sugar
1 Tablespoon vinegar
1/2 teaspoon mustard
1/8 teaspoon tabasco sauce
1/2 teaspoon worcestershire sauce
1/2 green pepper, diced
1/2 onion, finely minced
1 clove garlic, finely minced
4 to 8 cups cooked pork roast, trimmed and shredded
1/2 teaspoon ginger
1/2 teaspoon allspice
1/2 teaspoon cloves
1/2 teaspoon pepper
small piece of cheese cloth

Preheat oven to 300°. Pour the contents of the ketchup bottle into a large, ovenproof pot. Take the 1/2 cup of water, fill the empty ketchup bottle with it, and pour that into the pot. Add sugar, vinegar, mustard, tabasco, and worcestershire to pot, and mix thoroughly. Add the green pepper, onion and garlic. Mix and add pork, stirring until pork shreds are coated. Grind the spices, and tie them up in the cloth. Make a well in the center of the pot and add the bag of spices. Cover pot with heavy aluminum foil and place lid over the foil so that the fit is very tight. Bake at 300° for 1 hour. Remove from oven and stir. Bake for 1 more hour. Remove spice bag and serve. Great on almost any type of sturdy rolls or a pita pocket. Serve with cole slaw or potato salad.

LEFTOVER HAM IDEAS

1. Slice leftover ham into thin slices and pan fry as an accompaniment to fried eggs.
2. Cover a toasted, buttered, English muffin with a pan fried, thin slice of ham. Top with a poached egg and hollandaise sauce.
3. Make a sandwich of ham and Swiss on white bread. Dip sandwich into French toast batter and grill for a super Monte Cristo treat.
4. Dice ham into small cubes. Mix eggs and scramble together in the usual manner.
5. Mix scraps of ham into your favorite potato salad.
6. Add scraps of ham to scalloped potato casserole.
7. Add scraps of ham to canned split pea soup. Top with croutons.

COLD LAMB VINAIGRETTE

2 cups cooked lamb, cut into strips
2 cups green beans, cooked but firm
1 red onion, thinly sliced
1/4 cup fresh parsley, chopped

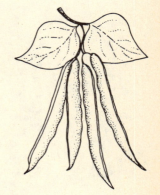

For the Vinaigrette:
1/4 cup red wine vinegar
1 Tablespoon dijon mustard
1 clove garlic, minced or pressed
1 teaspoon coarse salt
1/2 teaspoon pepper
3/4 cup olive oil

In a bowl, combine vinegar, mustard, garlic, salt, and pepper. Whisk, and add the oil in a steady stream. In a large bowl, combine lamb, green beans, red onion, and parsley. Pour vinaigrette over all. Allow to marinate for at least 1 hour. Serve on a bed of lettuce, something different such as arugula if available, and garnish with a row of uniformly sized green beans.

SAUTÉED LAMB SLICES

6 1/4" slices of cooked lamb
dijon mustard
12 to 14 saltines, crushed
clarified butter, enough to measure
    1/4" in a pan

Coat the lamb slices with mustard and saltine crumbs. Sauté the coated slices of lamb in a skillet in the clarified butter until brown on both sides. Garnish with very thinly sliced cucumber and a fresh mint leaf. Serve as a main course with rice and a green vegetable, or in French bread with lettuce or cucumber slices. I also love lamb with a side dish of good sliced red tomatoes and those salty Greek olives, with a little bit of Feta cheese sprinkled over the top.

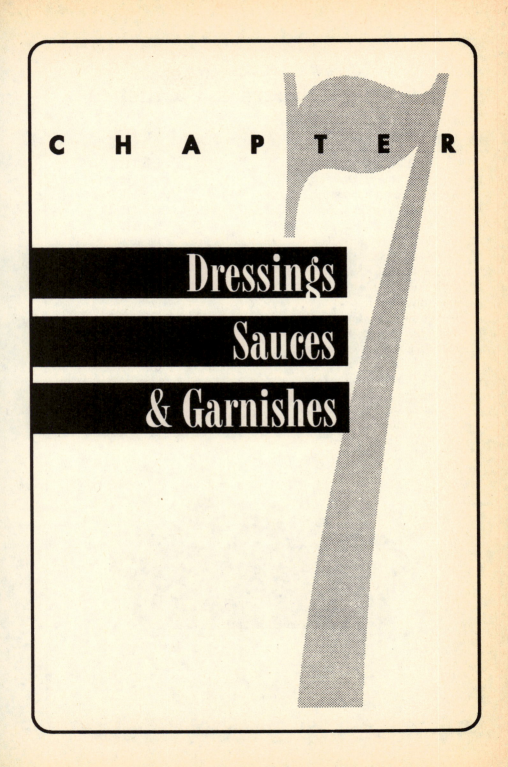

C H A P T E R

Dressings

Sauces

& Garnishes

7

THINGS TO COME IN...
Dressings, Sauces & Garnishes

VINAIGRETTE DRESSING

1/4 cup red wine vinegar
1 Tablespoon dijon mustard
1/4 teaspoon worcestershire sauce
1 clove garlic, minced or pressed
1 teaspoon coarse salt
1/2 teaspoon pepper
3/4 cup olive oil

In a bowl, combine vinegar, mustard, worcestershire sauce, garlic, salt, and pepper. Whisk together, and add the oil in a steady stream, whisking vigorously. Taste and adjust the seasonings.

AVOCADO SALAD DRESSING

1 cup avocado, mashed
2 Tablespoons onion, chopped
1/4 Tablespoon lemon juice
1/2 cup buttermilk
1/3 cup mayonnaise
pepper to taste
1/2 teaspoon coarse salt

Combine all of the ingredients in a blender or food processor, and process until smooth. Taste and adjust seasonings

BLUE CHEESE DRESSING I

2 Tablespoons sharp blue cheese, crumbled
1/2 cup sour cream
1/2 cup mayonnaise
1 teaspoon dried dill seed
1 small clove garlic, crushed
1/4 teaspoon pepper

Combine all of the ingredients in a blender or food processor, and process until smooth. Taste and adjust seasonings.

BLUE CHEESE DRESSING II

2 Tablespoons red wine vinegar
1 teaspoon dijon mustard
1 Tablespoon parsley, finely chopped
1 small clove garlic, put through a press
1 teaspoon coarse salt
1/4 teaspoon pepper
1/4 cup salad oil
2 Tablespoons sharp blue cheese, crumbled

Combine vinegar, mustard, parsley, garlic, salt, and pepper in a bowl.
Beat with a whisk until thickened. Add the oil in a steady stream,
beating constantly. Stir in the cheese.

CHAMPAGNE DRESSING

1 cup mayonnaise
1/3 cup heavy cream
1/3 cup flat, dry champagne
1 clove garlic, put through a press
1/4 teaspoon dried dill weed
1 teaspoon dijon mustard
salt & pepper to taste

Thin mayonnaise with heavy cream. Whisk in champagne. Add
garlic, dill, mustard, salt, and pepper. Mix thoroughly and allow to
stand for a few minutes. Use to dress bib or boston lettuce leaves.

SAUCES

Sauces play a crucial role in cooking with leftovers. A good
hollandaise can turn leftover broccoli into sumptuous fare, while
bechamel sauce can make scraps of steak a gourmet meal. It is
important to remember though, that a sauce should enhance the true
quality of food, not mask its flavor. If the veggies are too soggy or the
meat too dry, a sauce can be a waste of time and resources. It is also
important not to over use sauces. Too many rich sauces at one meal

is unappetizing. Instead, serve a fresh salad or a good crusty bread along with a sauced main dish, so that a palateable balance is achieved.

Thickening agents for sauces are usually eggs and flour, but they each must be handled with care, as eggs curdle and flour lumps. To avoid this, beat eggs together first, add a few spoonfuls of the hot liquid to the yolks, stirring rapidly, and then add the egg mixture to the sauce. Stir the complete sauce thoroughly, and when you are adding the eggs, always use a wooden spoon, as metal tends to discolor the yolks. If you are making a sauce that must stay hot for a long time, add flour as your thickener instead, as it is difficult to prevent the eggs from cooking if they are heated for too long.

In the case of flour, mix it with the liquid it is thickening first, and then add the mixture to the sauce, removing the pan from the heat source before you add any liquid. Then stir constantly to prevent lumping. Once mixed in thoroughly, put back on the heat, and continue to stir. Another option is to remove the sauce to the top of a double boiler and make the sauce over simmering water in order to avoid burning it.

BECHAMEL SAUCE I

4-1/2 Tablespoons butter
7-1/2 Tablespoons flour
3 cups milk, scalded
salt & pepper to taste

In a heavy saucepan, melt the butter. Add flour, stirring constantly for 2 minutes. Add scalded milk to the roux by whisking vigorously. Cook, stirring constantly, until thick and smooth. Turn heat to low and simmer for 10 minutes. Season with salt and pepper. This is a basic white sauce, and can be the basis of a number of others. Experiment. Just add ingredients as you see fit.

BECHAMEL SAUCE II

4-1/2 Tablespoons butter
4-1/2 Tablespoons flour
3 cups strong chicken stock, scalded
3/4 cup parmesan cheese, grated
1/2 teaspoon tarragon
salt & pepper to taste

Melt butter over low heat, blending in flour and whisking for about 2 minutes. Remove from heat. Add the stock to the flour mixture all at once, whisking vigorously. Set pan over high heat and keep whisking until it comes to a boil. Lower heat and simmer for about 5 minutes. Add cheese and stir until it melts. Remove pan from heat and add tarragon, salt, and pepper to taste. This should make about 3 cups of sauce.

MORNAY SAUCE

2 Tablespoons butter
2 Tablespoons flour
1 cup milk
3 Tablespoons heavy cream
3 Tablespoons Swiss or
    parmesan cheese, grated
salt & pepper to taste

Melt the butter in a heavy saucepan, and blend in the flour. Remove the pan from heat, and slowly add the milk and heavy cream. Add the grated cheese. Blend until smooth. Season to taste with salt and pepper. This is a wonderful sauce to top any hearty, leftover vegetable.

HOLLANDAISE SAUCE

8 Tablespoons butter
3 egg yolks
2 teaspoons lemon juice
a few grains cayenne pepper
salt & pepper to taste

Melt butter in a small saucepan. In a blender, combine yolks, lemon juice, and cayenne. Turn blender on and off quickly, twice. While butter is hot, and with the blender on high, pour melted butter in a steady stream into the egg mixture until the butter is all blended and the sauce has thickened. Add salt and pepper to taste. Let sit at room temperature for 5 minutes to further thicken before serving. For some variety, try adding a 1/2 teaspoon of tarragon (Bernaise sauce) or 1/4 teaspoon dry mustard. This sauce is so easy to make, it seems a crime not to lavish all leftovers in it!

SAUCE DIABLE

2 Tablespoons butter
1 medium onion, finely chopped
1/2 cup beef stock
1/2 cup dry red wine
1 teaspoon dijon mustard
2 Tablespoons worcestershire sauce
1-1/2 teaspoons cornstarch
salt & pepper to taste
dash of lemon juice

In a heavy skillet over moderate heat, melt butter and cook the onion until soft and transparent. Do not let the onion brown. Add the stock, wine, and all the seasonings except the lemon juice. Cook until hot. Add the dash of lemon juice just before serving.

SOUBISE SAUCE

3 Tablespoons butter
1 large onion, chopped
1 cup cooked rice
1-1/2 cups chicken stock
6 mushrooms
1 egg yolk
1/4 cup cream
salt & pepper to taste

In a saucepan, melt the butter and sauté the onion until it is soft. Do not brown. Add rice and chicken stock. Bring to a boil and let simmer for 5 minutes. Cook mushrooms in a saucepan with enough water to cover them and simmer for 5 to 10 minutes. Drain thoroughly. In a blender or food processor, combine rice mixture, mushrooms, egg yolk, and cream. Process until smooth. Add salt and pepper to taste. Remove to the top portion of a double boiler over simmering water until ready to serve. This is a rich and tasty sauce to pour over almost any plain, leftover, sliced meat.

PASTA SAUCES

Pasta is a woderful way to get rid of leftovers. Just boil up some noodles, or reheat those that are leftover, and top with a creative dressing or sauce containing various leftover vegetables, fish, poultry, or meats. Good cold dressings to toss over pasta and leftovers are vinaigrettes and avocado, (see page 117) and cold pesto. The three basic warmed pasta sauces are a red, or tomato base, a white, or cream base, and a plain butter base. Each is delicious, and can harbor any number of leftover meats or vegetables. Just add whatever sounds exciting.

BASIC TOMATO SAUCE

1 Tablespoon butter or olive oil
1 onion, diced
3 Tablespoons tomato paste
1 large can tomato sauce
3 large tomatoes, diced
1/3 cup red wine
1/2 teaspoon oregano
1/2 teaspoon basil
salt & pepper to taste

In a heavy saucepan, sauté the onion in the butter or oil over a medium flame. Add tomato paste and sauce, along with fresh tomatoes. Mix well. Add wine, turn heat down, and simmer for 10 minutes. Add seasonings and leftovers desired, and continue to simmer until desired consistency is reached. I like to add mushrooms and good Italian sausage. If meat is being used, and it is not precooked, you should sauté it first, and then sauté the onion and any vegetables in the fat drippings.

BASIC CRÈME SAUCE

3 Tablespoons butter or olive oil
1 onion, diced
1 cup heavy cream, or sour cream
1/3 cup white wine, or sherry
1/2 teaspoon tarragon
salt & pepper to taste

In a heavy saucepan, sauté the onion in the butter or oil over a medium flame. Add the cream and wine, and any desired leftovers and seasonings, and continue to sauté for another 10 minutes. I like to add mushrooms and shellfish to this sauce. A garnish of fresh parsley looks beautiful against the white sauce.

BASIC BUTTER SAUCE

8 Tablespoons butter
1 onion, diced
any leftover vegetables
1/2 teaspoon oregano
1/2 teaspoon basil
salt & pepper to taste

In a heavy saucepan, sauté the onion in the butter over a medium flame. Add other vegetables and seasonings, and sauté until heated through. The trick with this sauce is to use a variety of colors in your leftovers!

RYE CROUTONS

rye bread toast, buttered or dry
butter

If toast is dry, spread with melted butter. Cut bread into small squares. Place single layer on cookie sheet and bake in a 250° oven until brown and dry, about 30 minutes. Blot on paper towels to remove excess butter. Cool completely and store in an airtight container. Use in salads or soups.

STUFFINGS (see CASSEROLES, page 129)

PORK STUFFING FOR POULTRY (12 LB. BIRD)

4 cups stale bread, seasoned and cubed
1 cup chicken stock
4 cups pork, cooked or uncooked, ground
3 cloves garlic, chopped
1 cup onions, diced
1 to 1-1/2 cups mushrooms, coarsely chopped
1/2 cup celery, sliced
1 cup butter
1/4 cup dried fruit (optional)
1/4 cup apples (optional)
1/4 cup roasted nuts, sliced (optional)
2 eggs, lightly beaten

1/3 cup parsley, chopped
2 Tablespoons fresh rosemary
1 Tablespoon marjoram
1 Tablespoon sage
1 Tablespoon oregano
1 Tablespoon thyme

Preheat oven to 250°. Spread bread cubes on a jelly roll pan and toast bread at 250° until it is as dry as toast. Turn oven up to 350°. Put bread cubes in a deep bowl or pan. Coat bread in enough stock to make it soft in texture, but not soupy. Let soak. In a heavy pot, sauté the pork if uncooked, for 10 minutes until it is no longer pink. Remove the cooked pork with a slotted spoon, and add it to the bread cubes, leaving the grease in the pot. One batch at a time, sauté the garlic, onions, mushrooms and celery in the grease, adding butter as necessary. As each batch is cooked, add to the bread cubes and toss well. Add any optional fruit and/or nuts, and toss. Add eggs and seasonings. Mix well, taste, and adjust seasonings. Put stuffing in the cavity of the bird and cook as normal, or place it in a greased baking or roasting pan, cover it with foil, and bake at 350° for 1 hour.

RICE STUFFING FOR
PORK CHOPS OR POULTRY

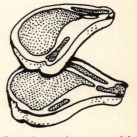

1/2 cup onion, finely minced
3 Tablespoons butter
1 Tablespoon curry powder
1 cup cooked rice
1/4 cup dried apricots, finely chopped
2 Tablespoons plain yogurt
apricot preserves

In a large skillet, sauté onion in butter until soft and translucent. Add curry powder and cook over low heat for 3 minutes, stirring occasionally. Add rice and stir. Add the apricots and yogurt. Mix. Fill cavity of bird with stuffing and cook according to directions. Or, slice pork chops open and pack with stuffing. Spread 1 Tablespoon of apricot preserves, jam or jelly on each chop, and broil for a few minutes, watching closely. Remove from oven and sprinkle fresh or dried chopped mint over the glazed chops.

CHAPTER

The
Main
Event

CASSEROLES

Casseroles are a wonderful way to to utilize a variety of leftovers. When making a casserole, vegetables, meats, and spices are usually bound with a mixture of egg, cheese, and rice or bread, and then baked in an ovenproof dish for 30 to 60 minutes, until browned and solidified. They are simple to make, have very little clean up, and are great for pot luck meals. The secret to a good casserole is to combine interesting colors and textures, and to pay close attention to the seasonings. The same is true for stuffings.

DIVINE CHEESE CASSEROLE

2 cups milk
3 eggs, lightly beaten
1/4 teaspoon salt
1/8 teaspoon paprika
pinch of cayenne pepper
1 teaspoon onion, grated (optional)
1 Tablespoon parsley or chives, chopped (optional)
1/4 teaspoon mustard (optional)
8 slices of bread, crusts trimmed off, cut diagonally in half
6 oz. processed cheese, any type, cut into 1/4" strips

Grease an 8" oven proof dish with butter or margarine. Add milk to eggs and beat well. Add salt, paprika, and cayenne. At this point, add optional onion, parsley or chives, and mustard. Put half of the bread in the bottom the prepared dish. Put cheese strips on top of the bread layer. DO NOT OVERLAP THE BREAD OR THE CHEESE! Put the rest of the bread over the cheese. Pour egg mixture over all. Let stand for 1 hour. Bake at 350° for about 1 hour, or until browned. Garnish with chopped ham or salami. Should be served at once.

TURKEY, RICE & MUSHROOM CASSEROLE

5 Tablespoons butter
2 medium onions,
    finely chopped
1 to 1-1/2 cups mushrooms,
    sliced
2-1/2 cups cooked
    turkey, cubed
1 cup leftover bread
    stuffing, crumbled
4 Tablespoons parsley,
    chopped
1 cup uncooked rice
2 cups hot chicken stock
2 Tablespoons dry sherry
salt & pepper to taste

Preheat oven to 350°. Grease a casserole dish with butter or margarine. Melt 4 Tablespoons butter in a skillet. Sauté the onions over medium heat until soft. Add the mushrooms and cook for 2 to 3 minutes. Combine the turkey, stuffing, mushrooms, onions, and parsley in the prepared casserole dish. Mix well and season to taste. This will vary according to how the stuffing was seasoned. Melt the remaining butter in the skillet and sauté the rice until it is just translucent. Add the rice to the casserole. Heat the stock and sherry together. Simmer for 5 minutes. Pour the liquid over the casserole. Mix well and cover the casserole tightly. Bake at 350° for 30 minutes, making sure rice is tender and liquid is absorbed. If the rice does not seem tender enough, add a little more heated stock and continue to cook.

LAMB & EGGPLANT CASSEROLE

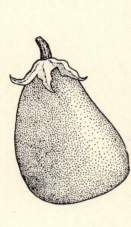

3 eggplants
1/4 cup flour
3 Tablespoons oil
3 Tablespoons butter
1 clove garlic, minced
3 Tablespoons onion, minced
1/2 cup mushrooms, chopped
1-3/4 cups cooked lamb, ground
2 eggs, lightly beaten
2 medium tomatoes, diced
2 Tablespoons fresh
    parsley, chopped
1 teaspoon oregano
1 Tablespoon salt
1/2 teaspoon pepper
1/2 cup bread crumbs
2 Tablespoons parmesan
    cheese, grated

Preheat the oven to 400°. Grease a 2 quart casserole dish with butter or margarine. Peel and dice 2 eggplants, and cook in boiling salted water for 15 minutes. Drain well and mash. Peel the third eggplant and cut into slices 1/2" thick. Coat with flour and brown on both sides in the oil. Reserve. Heat 2 Tablespoons butter and sauté the garlic, onion, and mushrooms until onion is limp. Combine this mixture with the eggplant pulp. Stir in the lamb, eggs, tomatoes, parsley, oregano, salt, and pepper. Place a 1" layer of eggplant and lamb mixture in the prepared casserole dish. Then place over that a layer of eggplant slices. Repeat until you run out of ingredients. Cover with bread crumbs and cheese. Dot with remaining butter. Bake at 400° for 30 minutes. Serve with tomato sauce and rice.

SPINACH & BEEF
FRITTATA

1/2 cup onion, minced
1 large clove garlic, minced
2 Tablespoons olive oil
1-1/2 Tablespoons butter
3 cups cooked beef, ground
1 cup cooked spinach, drained
    and chopped
1 teaspoon oregano
1/2 teaspoon salt
1/2 teaspoon pepper
5 eggs
1-1/2 teaspoons cornstarch
1 cup crème fraîche
3 cups whole milk
1/2 cup cheddar cheese, grated
1/4 cup gruyere cheese, grated

Preheat oven to 350°. Lightly butter a 12" x 9" x 2" baking dish. In a skillet, sauté the onion and garlic in olive oil until soft. Add the butter and quickly mix the beef with the onions and garlic. Add the spinach to the beef mixture and mix well. Season with oregano, salt, and pepper. Remove from heat. In a large bowl, beat the eggs with the cornstarch. Add the crème fraîche and milk. Mix thoroughly. Add the spinach and beef mixture to the eggs and mix. Add 1/4 cup of cheddar, and all the gruyere cheese. Gently mix together. Pour into prepared baking dish. Sprinkle the remaining cheddar cheese over the frittata. Bake at 350° for 55 minutes or until lightly brown and set. Cut into squares and serve. Any kind of potatoes would be a great side dish. Note: Feel free to change the two main ingredients ... frittatas are a classic vehicle for leftovers. Just use your imagination.

BREAD PUDDING GRUYERE

2 cups stale bread, cubed
4 Tablespoons melted butter
1 cup half and half
2 eggs, lightly beaten
1-1/2 cups gruyere cheese, cubed
1/4 cup parmesan cheese, grated

Preheat oven to 350°. Grease a casserole dish with butter or margarine. In a large bowl, toss bread cubes in melted butter. Combine cream and eggs and pour over bread cubes. Mix cheese cubes into bread mixture and pour into the prepared casserole. Bake at 350° for 45 minutes. Grated steamed zucchini would be a good garnish or side dish, or serve with a crunchy salad for contrast.

SAVORY SAUSAGE BREAD PUDDING

1 cup milk, scalded
2 cups stale bread, cubed
3 eggs
1/4 teaspoon salt
1/4 teaspoon pepper
1/4 teaspoon basil
1/4 teaspoon oregano
1 cup + 2 Tablespoons
      parmesan cheese, grated
1/2 cup cooked sausage
      meat, thinly sliced
1 tomato, peeled and thinly sliced

Preheat oven to 350°. Grease a 6" x 9" x 2" baking dish with butter or margarine. In a small bowl, pour milk over the bread cubes. Set aside. Mix the eggs with the seasonings and add the cup of parmesan cheese. Mix and then combine with bread cubes. Put half the bread mixture in the prepared baking dish. Cover with sausage slices and cover with tomato slices. Pour remainder of bread mixture over all. Top with 2 Tablespoons parmesan, and bake at 350° for 45 minutes or until puffy. Brown under a broiler, watching constantly until just brown and not blackened.

RICOTTA, SPINACH & BEEF PUDDING

1/3 cup shallots, minced
3 Tablespoons butter
1 cup cooked roast beef, ground
2 Tablespoons duxelles (optional)
10 oz. frozen spinach, thawed, chopped, and drained
1/3 cup sour cream
1/4 cup parsley, chopped
1 teaspoon oregano, ground
salt & pepper to taste
2 cups ricotta cheese
4 eggs
3/4 cup buttermilk
1/4 cup parmesan cheese, grated

Preheat oven to 325°. Grease a 1-1/2 quart baking dish with butter or margarine. In a heavy skillet, sauté shallots in butter for 2 minutes. Add beef, stirring constantly. Add duxelles and the spinach. Add more butter if necessary. Combine mixture completely and bind with sour cream. Add the seasonings and mix. Beat ricotta cheese with eggs until the mixture is well blended. Add the buttermilk to that, and then add the spinach and beef mixture. Adjust seasonings and pour into prepared baking dish. Sprinkle top with parmesan cheese. Put dish in a pan, adding enough water to reach halfway up the dish. Bake at 325° for 1 hour, until set. Run under broiler to brown the top. Serve with biscuits.

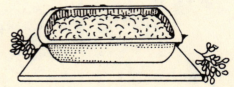

BROCCOLI PIE

4.5 oz. herb cheese such as boursin
2 eggs
1 cup cooked broccoli, coarsely chopped
1/4 cup parmesan cheese, grated
1/2 cup Swiss cheese, shredded
pepper to taste

Preheat oven to 350°. Grease a 9" glass or ceramic pie plate or quiche dish with butter or margarine. In a mixer, food processor, or blender, combine herb cheese and eggs just until well blended. Place broccoli in prepared dish, and pour egg mixture over broccoli. Stir in parmesan and Swiss cheeses, and season with pepper to taste. Bake at 350° for 30 to 40 minutes or until nicely golden brown. Garnish with chopped apple, leaving the skin on for color. Serve with a crusty French bread.

BEEF PIE PUFF

pastry for 1 pie crust
2 cups cooked steak or roast beef, ground
4 slices genoa or hard salami
1/2 medium onion
6 parsley sprigs
salt & pepper to taste
1 cup cheddar cheese, shredded
1/4 cup + 3 Tablespoons parmesan cheese, grated
3 eggs, lightly beaten
1 cup sour cream
1 cup heavy cream

Preheat oven to 425°. Line a 12" x 9" x 2" baking dish with pie crust pastry. Prick it with a fork, line it with tin foil, and fill with rice or beans. Bake at 425° for 10 minutes. Remove baking dish, and turn oven down to 375°. Remove foil and rice or beans from baking dish. In a food processor or meat grinder, combine beef, salami, onion, parsley, salt, and pepper, processing until ground and well mixed. Spread bottom of pastry with the beef mixture. Cover with cheddar and 1/4 cup parmesan cheese. Combine beaten eggs with sour cream and heavy cream. Pour egg mixture over the pie and sprinkle with the remaining 3 Tablespoons of parmesan. Bake at 375° for 1 hour until pie is puffed and brown. Let your appetite be your guide on accompaniments ... probably the best is a simple salad.

SHEPHERD'S PIE

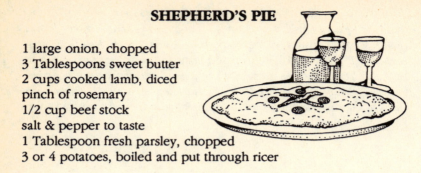

1 large onion, chopped
3 Tablespoons sweet butter
2 cups cooked lamb, diced
pinch of rosemary
1/2 cup beef stock
salt & pepper to taste
1 Tablespoon fresh parsley, chopped
3 or 4 potatoes, boiled and put through ricer

Preheat oven to 300°. Grease a shallow baking dish with butter or margarine. In a large skillet, sauté onion in sweet butter until wilted and golden. Stir in the lamb and rosemary. Add stock and season to taste. Cook until stock has cooked down to half its original volume. Turn into prepared baking dish and top with potatoes. Bake at 300° for 20 minutes, then run under the broiler for 1 or 2 minutes to brown the potato. Sprinkle with parsley. Serve with a small dish of buttered spinach.

POT PIE

2-1/2 cups cooked poultry or meat, cubed
1-1/2 cups mushrooms, thinly sliced
any leftover cooked vegetables, diced
2 Tablespoons parsley
1 cup baby sweet peas
2 Tablespoons butter
2 Tablespoons flour
2 cups milk, scalded
2 Tablespoons Madeira
1/2 teaspoon salt
1/4 teaspoon pepper
1/4 teaspoon nutmeg
1 prepared puff pastry crust
egg wash

Combine turkey, mushrooms, vegetables, parsley, and sweet peas. Make a sauce by heating butter and adding flour, cooking for 3 minutes. Do not let it color. Add scalded milk while stirring. Bring to a boil and cook, stirring until thick. Reduce heat, add Madeira and seasonings, and simmer for 10 to 15 minutes. Preheat oven to 375°. Combine sauce with turkey mixture and put it aside to cool. When cooled, put mixture into a pie dish and cover with puff pastry. To help crust adhere, place a moistened strip of pastry around the circumference of the dish and then cover with the crust. Crimp edges well, making slits for steam. Bake at 375° until golden brown. Brush top of pastry with egg wash and run under broiler for 1 minute.

TURKEY HASH

6 to 8 Tablespoons butter
1 small onion, diced
1/2 green pepper, diced
2 small potatoes, peeled, boiled and diced
2 cups cooked turkey, diced
3 slices crisp, cooked bacon, crumbled
salt & pepper to taste
1 egg
1 cup heavy cream
1/4 cup parmesan cheese, grated
1/4 cup gruyere cheese, grated

Melt 4 Tablespoons butter in a large heavy skillet. Over medium heat, sauté onions and green pepper until soft. Add potatoes to skillet. Cook until lightly brown. Add diced turkey and bacon to the vegetables and add more butter if needed to prevent mixture from sticking. Press down with spatula. Add salt and pepper to taste. Allow the hash to cook for about 10 minutes and then break up with a spatula. Combine egg, heavy cream and the cheeses in a bowl, then pour over the hash. Mix a bit and then cover and cook until the egg is set, 3 to 5 minutes. Turn out onto heated platter and serve immediately. Serve with spinach, sprinkled with grated parmesan cheese.

BEEF HASH

4 cups cooked roast beef, ground
1 10 oz. can tomato soup
1/2 cup ketchup
4 drops tabasco sauce
dash worcestershire sauce
1-1/2 cups (3 medium) potatoes,
 boiled and diced

Preheat oven to 375°. Combine ground meat with soup, ketchup, tabasco, and worcestershire sauces. Add diced potatoes and put all into a casserole. Smooth the top of the mixture. Bake at 375° for 1-1/2 hours or until brown and crusty. Serve with sour cream. Note: Steak or hamburger could also be used in this recipe.

HAM HASH AU GRATIN

1-1/2 Tablespoons shallots,
          minced
1 clove garlic, minced
2 Tablespoons unmelted butter
1 small green pepper, minced
1 cup mushrooms, chopped
1/3 cup chicken stock
1 teaspoon worcestershire sauce
1 cup cooked ham, chopped
salt & pepper to taste
1-1/2 cups cooked mashed potatoes
1 egg yolk
1/2 teaspoon paprika
1/4 cup parmesan cheese, grated
1/4 cup seasoned bread crumbs
1 Tablespoon melted butter

Grease a shallow baking dish with butter or margarine. Cook onion and garlic in 2 Tablespoons of unmelted butter until lightly browned. Add green pepper and mushrooms and cook for 4 minutes. Stir in chicken stock, worcestershire sauce, and ham. Season to taste, and mix. Bring to scalding point and keep hot. If using leftover potatoes, heat them slightly. Place mashed potatoes in pastry bag and pipe a border around the inner edge of the baking dish, or arrange as neatly as you can using a spoon. Brush egg yolk over potato border and sprinkle with paprika. Put ham mixture in the center of the baking dish and spread evenly. Combine grated cheese and bread crumbs and top the casserole with the mixture. Sprinkle top with 1 Tablespoon melted butter. Place in broiler about 6" from flame and broil until delicately brown. No need for a starch with this dinner ... just serve with a solid green vegetable such as asparagus, green beans, or brussel sprouts.

JAMBALAYA

2 slices crisp, cooked
  bacon, crumbled
1 small green pepper, diced
1/2 cup onion, chopped
1 Tablespoon flour
1-1/3 cups canned tomatoes
  with juice
3 cups cooked rice
1 cup cooked chicken, diced
1 cup cooked ham, diced
1/4 teaspoon thyme
1 teaspoon worcestershire sauce
salt & pepper to taste

After cooking the bacon, remove it to paper towels to drain, and in the same pan, cook the onion and green pepper until soft. Stir in the flour and mix well. Add the tomatoes and their juice. Bring to a boil, stirring frequently. Stir in the rice, bacon, and meats, add the seasonings, and heat for 10 minutes over a low heat. Serve as is, this is so colorful that it doesn't need any garnish.

STUFFED SAVOY CABBAGE

4 cups cooked beef, finely
    chopped
6 shallots, finely chopped
2 cloves garlic, minced
6 parsley sprigs, chopped
8 Tablespoons butter, melted
2 eggs, lightly beaten
1 large Savoy cabbage
1 large piece of cheesecloth
    to wrap cabbage
1 cup + 2 Tablespoons beef stock
1 bay leaf
1 carrot

Combine beef with shallots, garlic and parsley. Moisten meat mixture with butter and eggs. Place cabbage in a colander and pour boiling water over it. Gently pull the leaves away from the center, but don't pull them off. Cut center core out, making a well for the meat mixture. Drain cabbage upside down for a few minutes. Put cheese cloth on a work surface and place cabbage right side up in the middle of it. Stuff cabbage with meat mixture, starting in the center and working outward, putting filling between the leaves. Cabbage should look like a fat version of its original shape. Tie up with cheese cloth. Preheat oven to 275°. In a dutch oven, put beef stock, wine, bay leaf, and carrot. Bring to a boil and simmer for 1 or 2 minutes. Add cloaked cabbage, cover dutch oven tightly, and cook for 2 hours. Remove cheese cloth, put cabbage on a heated serving platter and strain pot juices over cabbage. Serve immediately with a wonderful crusty rye bread.

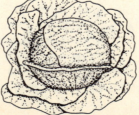

STUFFED EGGPLANT/ZUCCHINI

2 eggplants, or 4 zucchini
1 medium onion, minced
1 clove garlic, minced
3 Tablespoons butter
2 cups cooked beef or pork,
    ground or minced
1 cup tomatoes, chopped
1 Tablespoon parsley, chopped
1 Tablespoon salt
1/2 teaspoon pepper
4 Tablespoons parmesan
    cheese, grated
1 egg, lightly beaten
2 Tablespoons dried bread crumbs

Preheat oven to 350°. Grease a shallow baking pan with butter or margarine. Boil the eggplants, covered in a kettle for 15 minutes. If using zucchini, boil for 8 minutes. Drain and cut in half lengthwise. Remove the pulp, being careful to leave a 1/2" thick shell. In a skillet, sauté the onion and garlic in butter until onion is transparent. Chop the eggplant/zucchini pulp and add to skillet. Add the ground meat, tomatoes, parsley, salt, and pepper. Mix and remove from heat. Add 2 Tablespoons of parmesan and stir in the beaten egg. Fill the eggplant/zucchini shells with the mixture and place them in prepared baking pan. Sprinkle bread crumbs over the mixture and top with the remaining 2 Tablespoons of parmesan. Bake eggplant at 350° for 45 minutes, or zucchini at 350° for 25 minutes. Serve with any type of pasta, and tomato sauce over all.

RICE POISSON

1 Tablespoon butter
1 Tablespoon flour
1 cup milk, scalded
1/2 cup gruyere cheese, coarsely grated
salt & pepper to taste
1 cup cooked rice
7 oz. canned tuna, drained
2 hardboiled eggs, finely chopped
1/4 cup fresh parsley, chopped

Preheat oven to 350°. Grease a 1 pound mold with butter or margarine. Melt butter in a saucepan, add flour, and mix over low heat for 3 minutes taking care not to color the roux. Remove pan from heat and add scalded milk in a stream, whisking constantly. Return to heat and bring to a boil, stirring constantly. Lower heat and cook for 10 minutes, stirring occasionally. Stir in grated cheese, and remove from heat when melted. Season with salt and pepper. Combine the rice, tuna, eggs, and parsley in a small bowl. Gently add sauce to rice mixture and stir with fork. Pack into prepared mold. Cover top with a buttered round of waxed paper. Bake at 350° for 25 minutes or until heated through. Run a knife around the edge of the mold and turn out onto a heated serving dish. Sautéed green pepper is a good side dish, and some minced green pepper makes a pretty garnish.

KEDGEREE

1 teaspoon curry powder
salt & pepper to taste
3/4 cup heavy cream
2 cups tuna or other cooked fish, drained and flaked
2 cups cooked rice
4 hardboiled eggs, chopped
1/2 cup fresh parsley, chopped

Preheat oven to 350°. Grease a casserole dish with butter or margarine. Add seasonings to heavy cream and blend. Combine tuna with rice, eggs, and parsley. Add seasoned heavy cream to rice mixture and pack into the prepared dish. Cover with a buttered round of parchment or waxed paper and bake at 350° for 25 minutes, until heated through. Serve at once. Garnish with more of the chopped parsley and sprinkle with paprika.

FISH CURRY

4 Tablespoons butter
2 teaspoons curry powder
2 Tablespoons onion, minced
1 Tablespoon almonds or pine nuts
1/4 cup golden raisins, plumped in water, then drained
1 cup cooked fish, in pieces
2 cups cooked rice

Melt butter in skillet. Cook curry powder in butter over a low heat for 3 minutes, stirring constantly. Add onions and cook until wilted and translucent. Add nuts and cook until golden. Stir in raisins and remove from heat. Stir in rice with a fork. Add the fish and stir gently until coated. You can heat the mixture over a low heat until hot, and serve; or pack the rice into a buttered 2 cup mold, cover the top of mold with a buttered piece of waxed paper, and place mold on a rack in a pot with 2" of water. Cover pot and steam over a low heat until hot. Unmold onto a heated serving dish. Garnish with fresh chopped coriander. Another idea would be to set aside the cooked raisins and nuts and put a teaspoon of them on each serving.

CRAB & RICE SAUTÉ

8 Tablespoons butter
3 cups crabmeat, flaked
4 garlic cloves, pressed
1 box frozen artichoke hearts, thawed and drained
2-1/2 cups cooked rice
salt & pepper to taste
2 Tablespoons parsley, chopped

Melt butter in a skillet and sauté the crab over medium heat. Add the garlic and artichokes. Stir until well coated. Add rice and stir with fork, heating only until hot and no longer. Add salt and pepper, then sprinkle with parsley. Serve with hot sourdough bread.

FLORENTINE FISH

1/2 cup dry white wine
2-1/2 cups fish stock
8 Tablespoons butter
1 Tablespoon onion, finely minced
1/4 cup flour
1/4 cup heavy cream
1 cup mushrooms, thinly sliced
2 cups cooked fish
10 oz. frozen spinach, defrosted and drained
1/2 cup parmesan cheese, grated
salt & pepper to taste

Preheat oven to 350°. Grease a shallow baking dish with butter or margarine. Combine wine with 1/2 cup of fish stock. Bring to a boil and reduce by half. Reserve. Melt 4 tablespoons butter in a heavy saucepan and cook onions until soft. Add flour to form a roux and cook, stirring constantly, over a low flame for 3 minutes. Pour 2 cups of hot fish stock into roux and stir. Add reduced wine/stock mixture.

Thin sauce with heavy cream and stir in 3 Tablespoons butter, mixing well. Add salt and pepper to taste. Cook mushrooms in 1 Tablespoon of butter, then add them to the fish, and combine with the sauce. Spread the spinach over the bottom of the prepared baking dish, then spread the fish and mushroom mixture over it and top with parmesan. Bake at 350° for 20 to 30 minutes or until bubbly and hot. Place under a broiler for 1 minute, watching constantly to see that it browns and goes no further. You should serve rice with this or thin noodles to soak up the juices ... who would want to miss any of the cream, butter and wine?

HOT CHICKEN/TURKEY TIMBALE

1 cup warm chicken stock
1/2 cup light cream
4 eggs
salt & pepper to taste
1/2 teaspoon dried tarragon
1/2 cup Swiss cheese, grated
 1-1/2 cups cooked chicken or turkey, cut in large chunks

Preheat oven to 350°. Put the ingredients in a food processor and process for 10 to 20 seconds. Spoon the mixture into 6 buttered ramekins and set them in a pot of hot water. Bake at 350° for 25 to 30 minutes or until a knife inserted in the center comes out clean. Remove timbales from the oven and let stand for a few minutes to set. Run a knife around the edge and unmold. Serve immediately. Garnish with chopped pecans or walnuts. This makes a great luncheon dish, served with soft warm rolls and a salad.

APRICOT SOY CHICKEN

2 cups cooked chicken, skinned and cubed
1 15 oz. can of apricot halves (reserve juice for sauce)
1 Tablespoon peanut oil
1 teaspoon ginger, minced
2 hot peppers (or less to taste), seeded and dried
6 spring onions, sliced in rounds

For the Marinade:
1 clove garlic, crushed
1 Tablespoon corn starch
1/2 teaspoon pepper
1/2 teaspoon salt
1 Tablespoon soy sauce
2 teaspoons sesame oil

For the Sauce:
2 teaspoons cornstarch
1/2 cup apricot juice, from the can
1 Tablespoon soy sauce
1 Tablespoon apricot jam

Combine marinade ingredients and mix thoroughly. Mix chicken cubes into marinade and let stand for 30 minutes. Combine the sauce ingredients. Set aside. Cut apricots into strips. Heat oil in wok or frying pan. Add ginger and peppers and stir fry for 30 seconds. Add chicken and stir fry for 1 minute or until warm. Restir the sauce and add it to the pan. Add apricot slices and green onions, and sauté for 30 seconds. Turn out onto a serving platter and serve at once over rice. This would be made spectacular with the addition of fresh coriander.

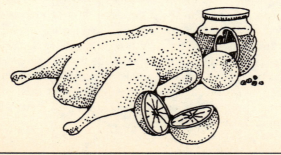

ALMOND CHICKEN

2 cups cooked chicken, cubed
2 Tablespoons peanut oil
1/2 teaspoon ground Szechuan peppercorns
2 cloves garlic, finely minced
2 teaspoons ginger root, minced
5 scallions, slant cut
4 whole hot peppers, seeded
10 oz. snow peas, fresh or frozen, defrosted and drained
1/2 cup whole roasted almonds

For the Marinade:
1 egg white
1 Tablespoon corn starch
1 Tablespoon sherry
1 Tablespoon soy sauce

For the Seasoning Sauce:
1 Tablespoon soy sauce
1 Tablespoon sherry
1 teaspoon sesame oil
1 teaspoon sugar
1 Tablespoon chicken stock
1 Tablespoon red vinegar, preferably Chinese
1 teaspoon corn starch

In a large bowl, mix together ingredients for marinade, add chicken, and refrigerate for 1 hour. Make seasoning sauce, set aside. Heat oil in frying pan or wok. Add chicken and cook for 1 minute. Remove to a platter, add peppercorns to the pan and brown for 1 minute. Add the garlic, ginger, scallions, and hot peppers, and stir fry for 1 minute. Add snow peas. Stir fry for 1 minute or until cooked but firm. Add the chicken and seasoning sauce and stir fry over a high flame for 2 more minutes. Add almonds and stir, then put all onto a heated platter and serve at once.

CHICKEN/TURKEY ELENA

For Rice:
4 Tablespoons butter
1 large onion, finely minced
1 clove garlic, finely minced
1 cup uncooked rice
2 cups chicken stock

For Poultry:
3 cups bechamel sauce (see page 119)
3 Tablespoons butter
1/2 to 3/4 cup mushrooms, thinly sliced
3 cups cooked chicken or turkey, diced
salt & pepper to taste
2 Tablespoons parmesan cheese, grated

To Make Rice:
In a skillet, melt butter, add the onion and garlic, and cook until the onion is transparent. Add the rice and sauté until golden. Place the rice mixture in a heavy saucepan, add the chicken stock, and cover with a tight fitting lid. Bring to a boil, reduce heat to the lowest point possible and simmer for 15 minutes. Let the rice sit covered and undisturbed for 20 minutes, then fluff with a fork before serving.

To Make Poultry:
Preheat oven to 400°. Sauté the mushrooms in 2 Tablespoons butter until soft. Add the chicken or turkey and bechamel sauce to the mushrooms and mix well. Season with salt and pepper if more is needed. In a rectangular baking dish, put a layer of rice, cover with a layer of chicken or turkey mixture, and repeat until all ingredients are used up. Sprinkle parmesan over all and dot with the remaining butter. Bake at 400° for 15 minutes or until hot in the center. A beautiful side dish would be sautéed red peppers.

CHICKEN/TURKEY TETRAZZINI

4 Tablespoons butter
1 to 1-1/2 cups mushrooms, thinly sliced
4 Tablespoons flour
2 cups chicken stock
1 cup heavy cream
salt & pepper to taste
1 Tablespoon fresh parsley, chopped
2 Tablespoons dry sherry
3 cups cooked chicken or turkey, cubed
1/2 cup slivered almonds
8 oz. fettucine, boiled and drained
1/2 cup dry bread crumbs
6 Tablespoons parmesan cheese, grated

Grease a shallow baking dish with butter or margarine. Melt butter in a heavy sauce pan and sauté the mushrooms until cooked but not brown. Stir in flour and mix until smooth. Add stock and cream, and whisk until boiling and thick. Simmer for about 10 minutes. Stir in salt, pepper, and parsley. Add the sherry, stirring constantly. Add the chicken or turkey and almonds and mix well. Place cooked fettucine in prepared baking dish and top with the poultry mixture. Sprinkle with bread crumbs and cheese. Brown under broiler and serve. If you have sun dried tomatoes on hand, dice them and sprinkle a bit on each serving.

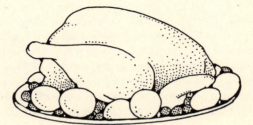

SPINACH & CHICKEN FILLED MANICOTTI

8 manicotti shells, cooked and drained

For the Filling:
1/2 cup onion, finely chopped
1 clove garlic, finely chopped
4 Tablespoons butter
1 cup spinach, cooked, drained and chopped
1/2 teaspoon salt
1/4 teaspoon pepper
1/4 teaspoon nutmeg
1 cup cooked chicken, finely diced
1 cup ricotta cheese
1/4 cup parmesan cheese, grated
3/4 cup heavy cream
1/4 cup parsley, chopped

For the Sauce:
1 Tablespoon onion, minced
3 Tablespoons butter
3 Tablespoons flour
1 cup milk, scalded
1 cup heavy cream
1/4 teaspoon salt
white pepper to taste
1/2 cup gruyere cheese, grated

For the Topping:
1/2 cup crème fraîche
2 Tablespoons parmesan cheese, grated
2 Tablespoons gruyere cheese, grated

To Make Filling:
In a heavy skillet, sauté onion and garlic in butter until onions are soft and lightly colored. Stir spinach in, using a fork if necessary to mix thoroughly. Add salt, pepper, and nutmeg. Add chicken, ricotta, and parmesan cheese, and stir the mixture until it is well combined. Stir in the heavy cream and simmer until it is reduced by half. Add the parsley, adjust the seasonings, and set aside to cool.

To Make Sauce:

In a heavy sauce pan, sauté the onion in butter. Do not color, cook only until onion is transparent. Add flour and stir the roux for 2 to 3 minutes. Add scalded milk and cream all at once and whisk until sauce is thick and smooth. Add salt and pepper to taste. Turn heat very low and simmer for 10 minutes, stirring frequently. Stir in cheeses and mix until melted. Remove from heat.

To Assemble:

Preheat oven to 375°. Grease an au gratin dish or a shallow rectangular 11" x 8" x 2" ovenproof serving dish with butter or margarine. Stuff cooked manicotti shells with filling using a butter knife or careful fingers. Arrange manicotti in the prepared dish (the shells should fit tightly). Cover manicotti with the sauce and cover with a thin layer of crème fraîche. Sprinkle cheeses over the crème fraîche. Bake at 375° for 20 minutes. Transfer the manicotti to a broiler for 2 minutes, sprinkle with chopped parsley, and serve at once.

RICE & BEEF BAKE

4 to 6 cups cooked beef, ground
8 Tablespoons butter
1 large onion, finely minced
4 cloves garlic, finely minced
1 to 1-1/2 cups mushrooms, sliced
24 oz. can Italian tomatoes
2 cups cooked rice
1-1/2 cups sharp cheddar cheese, grated
1/2 cup parmesan cheese, grated
1 teaspoon oregano
1 teaspoon basil
salt & pepper to taste
1/4 cup dry bread crumbs

Preheat oven to 350°. Grease a large baking dish with butter or margarine. In a large skillet, melt butter and sauté onion, garlic, and mushrooms. Add meat and tomatoes to mixture and simmer for 10 minutes. Break up tomatoes with a fork. Add rice, cheddar cheese, half the parmesan cheese, and the seasonings. Taste and adjust seasonings. Put mixture into prepared dish. Top with bread crumbs and remaining parmesan. Bake at 350° for 1 hour.

BEEF STROGANOFF

5 Tablespoons butter
2 Tablespoons flour
2 cups beef stock, scalded
2 teaspoons dijon mustard
1 clove garlic, minced
2 to 3 cups roast beef, cooked rare,
      trimmed, and cut into
      matchstick slices
1/4 cup dry sherry
1/2 cup sour cream, at room temperature
salt & pepper to taste
2 Tablespoons parsley, chopped
paprika

In a sauce pan, melt 3 Tablespoons of butter, add the flour and cook the roux, stirring constantly for 3 minutes. Add the scalded stock to the roux all at once, whisking vigorously. Sauté, stirring until thick and smooth. Add the mustard and simmer for about 10 minutes, stirring frequently. In another skillet, melt 2 Tablespoons butter and sauté the garlic until soft. Add beef strips. Remove beef to a heated platter as soon as it is warm. Deglaze the skillet by heating the sherry in it, and then pour it over the beef. Reheat the mustard sauce and stir in the sour cream. Cook over brisk heat for 3 minutes or until hot and thick. Do not boil. Add parsley, salt, and pepper. Put 1 cup of stroganoff sauce in a gravy dish. Put beef strips into remaining sauce. Serve on a bed of boiled rice or noodles. Sprinkle parsley over the top and shake paprika over each serving.

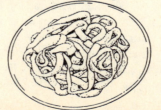

SLICED BEEF WITH GREEN PEPPERCORN SAUCE

2 Tablespoons butter
10 shallots, sliced
2 cups cooked beef or steak,
    thinly sliced
1/2 cup beef stock
1/4 cup heavy cream
1 teaspoon green peppercorns
1 Tablespoon dijon mustard
salt to taste

Melt the butter in a large skillet. Slowly sauté the shallots until soft and translucent but not brown. Add beef to shallots and quickly brown. Remove meat and shallots to a heated platter and keep warm. Over a medium heat, add beef stock, cream, and peppercorns to a saucepan. Bring to a boil and boil for 3 minutes, scraping up any brown bits that cling to the pan. Stir in mustard and cook 1 more minute. Pour over beef and serve immediately. Excellent served on toast with a simple vegetable such as peas.

DRAGON FILLET WITH SNOW PEAS

4 cups cooked beef, cut into matchstick slices
1/2 cup scallions, slant cut
10 oz. fresh or frozen snow peas, defrosted and drained
1 can water chestnuts, drained and sliced
2 cloves garlic, finely minced
1 cup frozen sweet peas, defrosted and drained (optional)
1/2 lb. string beans, slant cut and parboiled
2 cups fresh bean sprouts (optional)
2 Tablespoons peanut oil
1 Tablespoon cornstarch
1 Tablespoon sherry
1/3 cup chicken stock
1 Tablespoon hoisen sauce
1 Tablespoon bean sauce
2 teaspoons soy sauce
1/2 teaspoon salt
1/2 teaspoon sugar
1/4 teaspoon pepper
1/2 cup oven roasted almonds, blanched

To Prepare:
Put all vegetables and meat on a large preparation tray or roasting pan. Combine cornstarch and sherry in small bowl, mix well and place on preparation tray. Combine stock, hoisen, bean and soy sauces in another small bowl and add to preparation tray. Combine salt, sugar, and pepper in a third small bowl, and add to preparation tray.

To Cook:
Use a wok, electric fry pan or heavy iron skillet. Place pan over medium high heat for 30 seconds. Add peanut oil and heat for approximately 30 seconds until hot but not smoking. Add beef and stir fry 1 minute. Add string beans and stir fry 1 minute. Add garlic and scallions and stir fry 1 minute. Add bean sprouts and stir fry 30 seconds. Add water chestnuts and stir fry 30 seconds. Add snowpeas and peas and stir fry 30 seconds. Add salt, sugar, and pepper mixture. Add stock and sauce mixture and bring to a boil. Restir cornstarch and sherry and add while stir-frying, until mixture thickens. Empty contents of wok into a heated serving dish. Top with 1/2 cup oven roasted blanched almonds, and serve at once with boiled rice.

LAMB STEW

1 large onion, diced
2 cloves garlic, minced
1/4 cup olive oil
2 cups or more cooked lamb, diced
3 Tablespoons red wine vinegar
1 can tomato soup
1 cup dry sherry
1 cup cooked peas
salt & pepper to taste

In a deep saucepan, cook onion and garlic in olive oil. Add lamb and cook until warm. Add vinegar, tomato soup, and sherry. Heat until boiling. Add peas and cook over low heat for 5 minutes. Season with salt and pepper to taste. Serve with buttered and parsleyed new potatoes.

CURRIED LAMB WITH APPLES

3 Tablespoons butter
1 teaspoon curry powder
2 medium sized apples, peeled and diced
1 cup onion, minced
2 cups cooked lamb, diced
2 teaspoons flour
1 cup lamb or chicken stock, scalded
1 Tablespoon plain yogurt

In a heavy saucepan, melt the butter and add curry powder. Cook for 2 minutes, stirring. Add the apples and onions and cook for 5 minutes. Remove the apples and onions and add the lamb, browning it lightly. Remove the lamb, and stir flour into the pan juices to make a roux. Cook over low heat for 3 minutes. Add scalded stock and stir constantly until smooth and thick. Return all of the removed ingredients to the pan. Stir in the yogurt and adjust the seasonings. Serve over rice with French bread. Fresh coriander would make this an extra special dish.

LAMB WITH BLACK BEAN SAUCE

4 cups cooked lamb, trimmed and cut into matchstick slices

For Marinade:
2 Tablespoons dry sherry
1 Tablespoon light soy sauce
1 teaspoon sugar
1/2 teaspoon szechuan pepper, ground in a mill
1 teaspoon cornstarch
1 egg white, lightly beaten

For Seasoning Sauce:
2 Tablespoons dark soy sauce
4 Tablespoons dry sherry
2 teaspoons cornstarch
1 Tablespoon bean sauce
2 Tablespoons fermented black beans
3 cloves garlic, finely minced
2 teaspoons ginger root, finely minced
3 Tablespoons peanut oil
3 Tablespoons chicken stock
1 cup onions, thinly sliced
4 scallions (green and white part), shredded
4 dried hot peppers, seeds removed
1 cup ripe tomatoes, diced

Combine sherry, soy sauce, sugar, pepper, cornstarch, and egg white. Marinate lamb in mixture in refrigerator for at least 1 but not more than 12 hours.

Combine all of the ingredients for the seasoning sauce. Soak black beans in cold water for 10 minutes, drain and mince. Combine minced black beans with garlic and ginger.

Heat wok or heavy skillet until hot but not smoking. Add 1 Tablespoon peanut oil. Stir fry 1/2 the lamb until brown. Turn out on a heated serving plate. Add 1 Tablespoon of oil to wok and quickly stir fry the bean, garlic, and ginger mixture. Add the rest of the lamb and stir fry until brown. Empty contents of wok onto serving plate and add chicken stock to wok. Cook over moderate heat, scraping sides of wok with a spatula until a thick syrup is formed. Pour over meat. The entire dish can be prepared ahead of time up to this point.

Rinse wok with warm water only and return to heat. Add 1 Tablespoon of oil and heat until hot but not smoking. Stir fry onions, scallions and dried peppers for 2 minutes. Add tomatoes and stir fry for another minute. Add seasoning sauce and mix thoroughly. Add lamb mixture and stir fry over high flame until mixture is hot. Serve immediately.

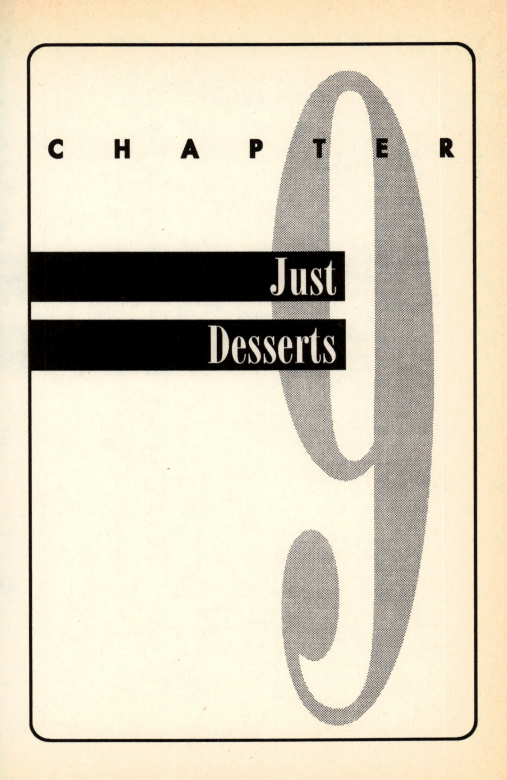

C H A P T E R

Just

Desserts

9

THINGS TO COME IN...
Just Desserts

ICE CREAM SAUCE

For a small amount of ice cream. Instead of refreezing, pour into small pitcher, place in refrigerator and use as a sauce for cake or soufflés.

PRESERVES SAUCE

1/4 cup cherry or apricot preserves
2 Tablespoons rum

Add rum to the preserves and heat the mixture until it is hot throughout. Great served over bread puddings, plain pound cake, rice pudding, etc.

PRESERVED WHIPPED CREAM

1 cup sweetened whipped cream which has started
to lose its stiffness and turn watery
2 Tablespoons apricot preserves

To each cup of whipped cream, stir in 2 Tablespoons apricot preserves. Works well as a dessert sauce.

HARD SAUCE

8 Tablespoons butter
1 cup confectioner's sugar
vanilla or liquor

In the work bowl of a food processor, cream butter until soft, and gradually add sugar, beating until smooth. Flavor with the vanilla or liquor.

EGGNOG SAUCE

1-1/2 teaspoons cornstarch
1 cup eggnog, scalded
2 egg yolks
1/4 cup sugar
1-1/2 teaspoons vanilla
1/4 teaspoon nutmeg

First mix cornstarch with 2 Tablespoons of scalded eggnog, and then add the rest of the scalded eggnog to the cornstarch mixture, whisking vigorously. Cook mixture, stirring constantly over a low heat until mixture lightly coats the back of a wooden spoon. In a separate bowl, beat eggs and sugar until light and fluffy. Add vanilla and nutmeg to the egg mixture. Remove cornstarch mixture from heat and add egg mixture. Return to heat and cook for 5 minutes or until sauce thickens. Cool at room temperature. Cover top of sauce with plastic wrap and chill.

VANILLA SAUCE

1-1/2 teaspoons cornstarch
1 cup whole milk
2 egg yolks
1/4 cup sugar
1-1/2 teaspoons vanilla

Moisten and mix the cornstarch with 2 Tablespoons of the milk. Heat the rest of the milk and add the cornstarch mixture. Cook the milk mixture over a low heat, stirring constantly until mixture lightly coats the back of a spoon. In a separate bowl, beat eggs and sugar until light and fluffy. Add vanilla to egg mixture. Remove the cornstarch mixture from the heat and add the egg mixture. Return to heat and cook for 5 minutes or until sauce thickens. Cool at room temperature for 1 hour, cover top of sauce with plastic wrap, and chill. Serve cold.

SABAYON SAUCE

4 egg yolks
1/4 cup sugar
1/4 cup Grand Marnier
1/2 cup heavy cream, whipped

In the top of a double boiler, beat egg yolks with electric mixer at medium speed, until thick. Beat in sugar, 1 Tablespoon at a time. Continue beating until mixture is light and soft peaks form when beater is slowly raised. Place double boiler on top of simmering water. DO NOT LET WATER TOUCH THE BASE OF THE DOUBLE BOILER TOP. Slowly, 1 Tablespoon at a time, beat in Grand Marnier. Continue beating for about 5 minutes or until mixture is fluffy. Set double boiler top in ice water. Beat custard until cool. Fold in whipped cream. Refrigerate covered, until cold.

ICED CRANBERRY CREAM

1 cup leftover orange-cranberry relish
1/3 cup superfine sugar (amount of sugar depends upon
    sweetness of relish)
1 Tablespoon Cointreau
1-1/2 cups heavy cream
4 egg whites

Heat relish with sugar and Cointreau until sugar melts. Test for sweetness. Add sugar if mixture is too tart. Cool. Beat cream until stiff. Combine cream and relish mixture thoroughly. Whisk egg whites until they hold soft peaks. Fold egg whites gently but thoroughly into cranberry mixture and turn out into a 1-1/2 quart soufflé dish. Freeze for 6 hours. Unmold and return to freezer until serving time.

COFFEE BUTTER CREAM

1-1/2 cups sweet butter
3 cups confectioner's sugar, sifted
4 egg yolks
2 teaspoons vanilla
2 teaspoons powdered coffee

Beat butter until light and fluffy. Add confectioner's sugar and continue to beat until light and fluffy. Add egg yolks, vanilla, and powdered coffee. Beat until smooth and glistening.

BREAD CRUMB CRUST

1-1/2 cups dry bread crumbs, toasted and sifted
6 Tablespoons butter, melted
1/4 cup confectioner's sugar, sifted

Combine bread crumbs, butter, and sugar. Pat mixture into pie pan and bake at 300° for about 15 minutes. Cool before filling.

COCONUT CRISPS

6 slices of bread, crusts removed,
        each cut in 4 strips
1 14 oz. can sweetened condensed milk
2-1/2 cups sweetened coconut, flaked

Preheat oven to 375°. Grease a baking sheet with butter or margarine. Using 2 forks, roll bread strips in milk, coating all sides. Using the same method, roll in coconut. Place strips on prepared baking sheet. Bake at 375° for 8 to 10 minutes until golden brown. Remove at once from baking sheet.

MOLDED APRICOT FRUIT

3 oz. box apricot jello
1 cup hot water
3/4 cup liquid from canned fruit
1 Tablespoon lemon juice
1/2 cup sour cream
1-1/2 cups canned fruit, chopped
1/2 cup pecans, chopped

Dissolve jello in water. Add fruit liquid and lemon juice. Place jello, sour cream, and 1/2 cup chopped fruit in blender. Mix thoroughly, pour into a bowl, and chill for 45 minutes. Remove from refrigerator and mix in nuts and remainder of fruit. Pour into an oiled mold. Refrigerate for 4 to 5 hours. Turn out on serving platter and garnish with fruit.

INDIVIDUAL PANCAKE CAKES

leftover pancakes, preferably thin and of uniform size
apricot or strawberry jam
confectioner's sugar
almonds, toasted and sliced

Preheat oven to 300°. Use three or more pancakes per cake, per person. Place pancake on sheet of foil. Spread jam liberally over surface of pancake. Cover with next pancake and spread with jam. Continue in this manner, making as high a stack as you wish, but not so high as to become unbalanced. Cover completely with foil and bake at 300° for 15 minutes. Unfold foil, and with a spatula, lift cake to a small dessert plate. Sprinkle liberally with confectioner's sugar and place toasted almonds on top. Serve with whipped cream flavored with a few teaspoons of the jam used in the pancake cakes.

INDIVIDUAL RUM CAKES

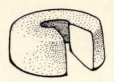

3 1/2" slices of pound cake per serving
1 teaspoon dark rum per slice
apricot jam
sweetened whipped cream
almonds, toasted and sliced

Sprinkle each piece of pound cake with rum. Spread each layer of cake with jam and put the layers on top of one another. Completely mask rum cake with whipped cream and refrigerate for 30 minutes. Just before serving, sprinkle top with toasted almonds.

LEFTOVER POUND CAKE TIPS

The last few slices

1. Toast and spread with red currant jam.
2. Toast and top with a scoop of ice cream covered with
      hot fudge sauce.
3. Toast and cover with macerated fruits.

SOUFFLÉS (see SOUFFLÉS page 85)

FROZEN CRANBERRY SOUFFLÉ

3/4 lb. cranberries
1-1/2 cups superfine sugar
3 Tablespoons Cointreau
1-1/2 cups heavy cream, whipped stiff
3 egg whites
1/8 teaspoon cream of tartar
pinch salt
3 Tablespoons sweet orange marmalade
1 cup sweetened heavy cream, whipped
orange zest, grated

Cook the cranberries with the sugar in a covered saucepan over a low heat for 10 minutes, stirring once or twice. Remove lid and cook for 5 minutes more. Add Cointreau and allow the mixture to cool. Fold the whipped cream into the cranberry mixture. Beat the egg whites with the cream of tartar and a pinch of salt until stiff. Fold them into the mixture. Pour into a 1-1/2 quart soufflé dish, cover with foil, and freeze for 6 hours. Turn out on a cold platter and return to the freezer for 1 hour. Make sauce by adding sweet orange marmalade to sweetened, whipped heavy cream. Remove soufflé from freezer, sprinkle the top with grated orange zest, and serve with sauce.

ORANGE-CRANBERRY
RELISH SOUFFLÉ

6 egg whites
pinch of salt
1/4 teaspoon cream of tartar
1/3 cup superfine sugar
2 cups leftover orange-cranberry relish, puréed
2 Tablespoons sweet orange marmalade

Preheat oven to 400°. Prepare a 1-1/2 quart soufflé dish by buttering a paper collar folded in half. Tie the paper, buttered side inward, so it rises 3" to 4" above the rim. Butter the inside of the soufflé dish and sprinkle it with sugar to coat the bottom and sides completely. Beat the egg whites until they are foamy. Add the salt and cream of tartar and continue beating until they form soft peaks. Gradually beat in sugar and continue to beat until the whites stand in stiff glossy peaks. Fold in the cranberry purée and sweet orange marmalade, incorporating it lightly but completely. Turn into the prepared soufflé dish. Smooth the top and bake at 400° for 25 to 30 minutes.

PEAR SOUFFLÉ

2 cups pears (4-6 pears),
    peeled and cubed
lemon juice
1 cup water
1 cup sugar
1/3 cup raspberry jam
1 teaspoon cornstarch
1 Tablespoon cold water
2 teaspoons superfine sugar
6 egg whites
1/4 teaspoon cream of tartar
pinch of salt
1/3 cup superfine sugar

To prevent pears from darkening, brush with lemon juice. Boil the water and 1 cup of sugar together for 3 minutes, stirring until the sugar has dissolved. Add the pear cubes, lower the heat and simmer until the pears are tender. Cool the pears in the syrup, then drain well. Purée the pear cubes in a blender, food processor, or through a fine sieve. Heat the jam, stirring until softened, then strain it. Mix the cornstarch with the cold water and add to the strained jam. Bring to a boil, stirring constantly, then cool. Combine the cooled raspberry jam mixture with the pear purée. Preheat the oven to 400°. Prepare a 1-1/2 quart soufflé dish with a paper collar. (See *Orange-Cranberry Relish Soufflé* on page 169 for details). Butter dish and collar and dust with the 2 teaspoons of superfine sugar. Beat the egg whites until they are foamy. Add the cream of tartar and pinch of salt. Continue beating until they hold soft peaks. Gradually add 1/3 cup of superfine sugar, 1 Tablespoon at a time, until the whites stand in glossy peaks. Fold the pear purée into the whites, incorporating it gently but completely. Turn into the prepared soufflé dish. Smooth the top and bake at 400° for 25 to 30 minutes.

HOLIDAY SOUFFLÉ

1/2 cup candied fruit, chopped
1/4 cup candied cherries, halved
2 Tablespoons light rum
3 Tablespoons sweet butter
3 Tablespoons flour
1-1/4 cups eggnog, scalded
1/2 cup sugar
4 egg yolks, lightly beaten
1/4 teaspoon nutmeg, grated
1 teaspoon vanilla
1/8 teaspoon cream of tartar
pinch of salt
5 egg whites

Preheat oven to 400°. Butter a 4 cup soufflé dish, and coat the bottom and sides in sugar. In a small bowl, marinate the mixed fruit and candied cherries in the rum. Melt the butter in a heavy saucepan and add the flour. Whisk together for 2 to 3 minutes over a very low flame. Do not allow roux to color. Add scalded eggnog all at once to roux and whisk vigorously until the mixture is thick and smooth. Add the sugar and mix thoroughly. Remove from heat and beat in the egg yolks, one at a time. Add the nutmeg and vanilla. Stir in the chopped fruit and halved cherries with the rum they were soaking in. In a mixing bowl, add cream of tartar and a pinch of salt to the egg whites, and beat until stiff. Fold the sauce into the egg whites, gently but thoroughly. Pour mixture into prepared soufflé dish. Place in oven, immediately lower temperature to 375°, and bake for 20 minutes. Serve immediately with sweetened whipped cream or a good rum sauce.

BAKED RICE PUDDING

2 eggs, lightly beaten
6 Tablespoons sugar
1/2 cup cottage cheese, creamy
1/8 cup cream cheese, whipped
3/4 cup sour cream
1/2 teaspoon vanilla
1/3 cup golden raisins
1-1/2 cups cooked rice
cinnamon
2 teaspoons butter
ground nutmeg or ground walnut

Preheat oven to 350°. Grease a casserole dish with butter or margarine. Mix eggs with sugar, and beat in the cottage cheese and cream cheese. Add sour cream, vanilla, and raisins. Stir cooked rice into mixture and pour into prepared casserole dish. Sprinkle top with cinnamon and dot with butter. Bake at 350° for 30 minutes, or until set. Sprinkle with a small amount of nutmeg, or finely ground walnut. Serve with vanilla sauce (see page 162), as this is a "dry rice pudding."

TRADITIONAL BREAD PUDDING

3 eggs
1/2 cup sugar
1 teaspoon vanilla
1/4 cup cream cheese, whipped
1 cup cottage cheese, creamy
1 cup heavy cream
3/4 cup sour cream
1/3 cup raisins
1 cup stale bread cubes, crustless
cinnamon
sugar
2 teaspoons butter

Beat eggs and add sugar. Beat until fluffy and lemony in color. Add vanilla. Beat in cheeses, creams and raisins. Mix. Add bread cubes and let sit for 20 minutes. Preheat oven to 350°. Butter a 1-1/2 quart casserole and pour bread mixture into it. Sprinkle top with cinnamon and sugar, and dot with butter. Bake at 350° for 45 minutes or until nicely browned and puffy. Serve at room temperature with a vanilla sauce (see page 162). If you serve the pudding with ice cream or whipped cream, dust that with the cinnamon and sugar as well.

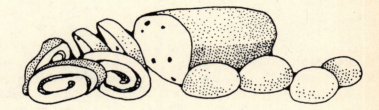

COFFEE CAKE PUDDING

1 egg
2 egg yolks
1/2 cup sugar
1 teaspoon vanilla
1 cup milk
2 cups coffee cake, cubed
1/2 cup candied
    cherries, halved
1/2 cup golden raisins
1/2 cup pecans, chopped

Grease a 1 quart casserole dish with butter or margarine. Beat egg, yolks, and sugar until light and fluffy. Beat in vanilla and milk. Combine cake, cherries, raisins, and nuts. Cover cake mixture with egg mixture and turn into casserole. Let sit for 30 minutes. Preheat oven to 350° and bake for 45 minutes or until set.

BREAD PUDDING WITH WHISKEY SAUCE

2 Tablespoons butter, softened
12 oz. loaf of day old French or Italian bread
4 cups milk
3 eggs
2 cups sugar
1/2 cup raisins
2 Tablespoons vanilla extract

For Sauce:
8 Tablespoons butter
1 cup sugar
1 egg
1/2 cup bourbon

To Make Pudding:

Preheat oven to 350°. With a pastry brush, spread the softened butter evenly over the bottom and sides of a 13" x 9" x 2" baking dish. Break the bread into chunks, dropping them into a bowl as you proceed, and pour milk over them. When the bread is softened, crumble it into small bits and let it continue to soak until all the milk is absorbed. In a small bowl, beat the eggs and sugar with a whisk or rotary beater until the mixture is smooth and thick. Stir in raisins and vanilla, then pour the mixture over the bread crumbs and stir until all the ingredients are well combined. Pour the bread pudding into the prepared baking dish, spreading it evenly and smoothing the top with a rubber spatula. Place the dish in a large shallow roasting pan set on the middle shelf of the oven and pour boiling water into the roasting pan to a depth of about 1". Bake at 350° for 1 hour or until a knife inserted in the center of the pudding comes out clean.

To Make Sauce:

Melt butter in the top of a double boiler set over hot but not boiling water. Beat sugar and egg together in a small bowl and add the mixture to the butter. Stir for 2 or 3 minutes, until the sugar dissolves and the egg is cooked, but do not let the sauce come anywhere near a boil or the egg will curdle. Remove the pan from heat and let the sauce cool to room temperature before stirring in the bourbon. Serve pudding at once, directly from the baking dish, and present the whiskey sauce separately in a sauce boat or a small bowl.

CHOCOLATE BREAD PUDDING

2 eggs
2 egg yolks
1 cup sugar
1 teaspoon vanilla
1 teaspoon strong brewed coffee
2 oz. unsweetened chocolate, melted
2 cups cream, half and half, or milk, scalded
2 cups bread cubes, crustless and stale
1/2 cup walnuts, chopped
confectioner's sugar

Preheat oven to 350°. Generously grease a shallow rectangular baking dish with butter or margarine. Mix eggs and yolks, and beat until light and fluffy. Gradually add sugar to the egg mixture while beating constantly. Add vanilla, coffee, and melted chocolate to egg mixture. Pour scalded cream over bread cubes. Combine egg and bread mixture. Stir in chopped nuts and pour into prepared baking dish. Bake at 350° for 50 minutes or until set. Sprinkle with confectioner's sugar, and serve warm. Naturally, this would only benefit by adding whipped cream or ice cream to the top!

APRICOT BREAD PUDDING

1 cup half and half, scalded
2 cups stale bread cubes
4 eggs
1 cup sugar
1 teaspoon vanilla
1 cup dried apricots, halved
1/2 cup pecans, coarsely chopped
cinnamon
3/4 cup apricot preserves
3 Tablespoons light rum

Preheat oven to 350°. Generously grease a shallow rectangular baking dish with butter or margarine. In a large bowl, pour scalded half and half over bread. In a separate bowl, combine eggs and sugar, beating until light and fluffy. Add vanilla, apricots and nuts to the egg mixture. Mix well. Combine egg mixture with bread, and pour into prepared baking dish. Sprinkle cinnamon over the top. Bake at 350° for 1 hour or until set. Combine apricot preserves and rum. Mix with an electric beater or put in a blender. Pour apricot glaze over baked pudding. Allow to rest for 30 minutes before serving. Serve with vanilla ice cream or sweetened whipped cream.

FRUITED BREAD PUDDING

2-1/2 cups buttered bread crumbs
1 cup canned fruit, chopped and drained
4 eggs
3 cups milk
3/4 cup sugar
1 teaspoon vanilla
1/2 cup pecans, chopped
cinnamon
sugar
2 teaspoons butter

Preheat oven to 375°. Grease a 1-1/2 quart casserole dish with butter or margarine. Place a layer of bread cubes on the bottom of the casserole dish. Cover with a layer of fruit and continue alternating until all ingredients are used up. Beat eggs, milk, sugar, and vanilla together. Pour mixture over bread and fruit and let rest for 30 to 60 minutes. Sprinkle the top with chopped nuts, cinnamon, and sugar. Dot with butter. Bake at 375° for 1 hour or until brown. Serve with sweetened whipped cream.

CANDIED FRUIT PUDDING

4 cups stale coffee cake, cubed
1 cup mixed candied fruit
1/2 cup candied cherries, halved
1/2 cup golden raisins, plumped and drained
1 cup walnuts, chopped
2 cups milk, cream or a combination, scalded
6 eggs, lightly beaten
1-1/2 cups sugar
2 teaspoons vanilla
1 teaspoon Grand Marnier

Preheat oven to 350°. Grease a large baking dish with butter or margarine. In a large bowl, combine coffee cake, candied fruits, raisins, and walnuts. Pour scalded milk over mixture. In a separate bowl, beat eggs with sugar. Add vanilla and Grand Marnier to egg mixture, pour over cake mixture, and mix thoroughly. Pour into prepared baking dish. Bake at 350° for 1 hour or until set and nicely browned. Serve with hard sauce (see page 161).

HOLIDAY BREAD PUDDING

2 cups eggnog, scalded
4 cups stale bread, cubed
4 eggs, lightly beaten
1 cup sugar
1 teaspoon vanilla extract
1/2 teaspoon nutmeg
1/2 cup candied mixed fruit
1/2 cup candied cherries
1/2 cup yellow raisins, plumped
1/2 cup pecans, chopped
1 Tablespoon butter
cinnamon

Preheat oven to 350°. Grease a rectangular baking dish with butter or margarine. In a large bowl, pour scalded eggnog over bread cubes, and soak. In a separate bowl, beat eggs and sugar until light and fluffy. Add vanilla and nutmeg to egg mixture, and stir in fruits and nuts. Add to bread mixture, and mix well. Pour mixture into prepared dish. Dot top with butter and sprinkle with cinnamon. Bake at 350° for 45 to 60 minutes until set. Serve hot with hard sauce (see page 161).

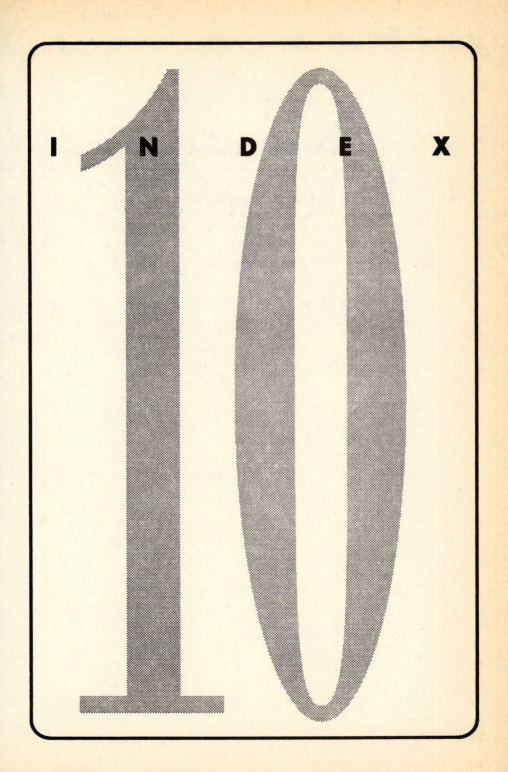

INDEX

THINGS TO COME IN...
Index

Due to the unusual nature of this book, and for ease and utility, the index is organized according to the main leftover ingredients for each recipe. Thus, find the category(ies) for leftover food which you have on hand, and scan the column for something that sounds interesting. The categories are organized according to food group, which facilitates the use of substitutions within a group ie: substitute pasta for rice, eggplant for zucchini, or apples for pears etc. Feel free to experiment and be creative.

RICE, PASTA & BEANS

BREADS, CRACKERS, CAKES & CEREALS

(Continued on next page.)

CHEESES

(Continued on next page.)

BEEF

HAM

PORK

LAMB

About the Authors

Patricia Rosier was a gourmet chef by trade and by calling. She began cooking in high school but became a serious chef in her twenties when she studied with James Beard. Raised in post World War II New York, Patricia learned early to respect food not only as a source of nourishment, but as a commodity for which to be thankful. She used food as a means of self expression, to show love to her adoring husband and two children, and to stimulate friends and strangers alike with her culinary creativity. Happily married for twenty two years, Pat had endless opportunities to test new recipes at parties hosted by her and her husband, Peter, in their Fort Myers, Florida home. Pat's untimely death in 1986 from lung cancer left those around her devastated. She is described as a woman mired in beauty, elegance, and charm who derived pleasure in life from caring for those around her. Now, her vivaciousness and generosity live on in the carefully presented recipes she created for *The Leftover Gourmet*.

Jessica Lauren Weiss, Research Director and Associate Editor for The Green Consumer Supermarket Guide and "The Green Consumer Letter", has been actively involved in a variety of food service projects for the past ten years. Studying under some of California's finest chefs, she has often fed hundreds of people at a time, catering for ABC during the 1984 Los Angeles Olympics, and for the U.C. Berkeley Food Service Department. Jessica has also used her enterprising mind to design menus and decor for restaurants. Particularly appalled by the rampant disposable consumerism of the eighties, Jessica devotes her life to researching how food can be more ecologically sound in its production, packaging, preparation, and consumption. She tests recipes in her Washington, DC home, where friends describe her as "an effervescent woman with a calling to feed". Jessica hopes everyone will enjoy helping out the planet by recycling with *The Leftover Gourmet*.